No Sail on the Western Sea

This book is edited and designed by the Editorial Committee of *Cultural China* series

Text by Ma Yuan
Translation by Tony Blishen
Cover Image by Getty Images
Interior Design by Xue Wenqing
Cover Design by Wang Wei

Editor: Wu Yuezhou
Editorial Director: Zhang Yicong

Senior Consultants: Sun Yong, Wu Ying, Yang Xinci
Managing Director and Publisher: Wang Youbu

ISBN: 978-1-60220-249-8

Address any comments about *No Sail on the Western Sea* to:

Better Link Press
99 Park Ave
New York, NY 10016
USA

or

Shanghai Press and Publishing Development Company
F 7 Donghu Road, Shanghai, China (200031)
Email: comments_betterlinkpress@hotmail.com

Printed in China by Shanghai Donnelley Printing Co., Ltd.

1   3   5   7   9   10   8   6   4   2

NO SAIL ON THE WESTERN SEA

By Ma Yuan

Better Link Press

Foreword

This collection of books for English readers consists of short stories and novellas published by writers based in Shanghai. Apart from a few who are immigrants to Shanghai, most of them were born in the city, from the latter part of the 1940s to the 1980s. Some of them had their works published in the late 1970s and the early 1980s; some gained recognition only in the 21st century. The older among them were the focus of the "To the Mountains and Villages" campaign in their youth, and as a result, lived and worked in the villages. The difficult paths of their lives had given them unique experiences and perspectives prior to their eventual return to Shanghai. They took up creative writing for different reasons but all share a creative urge and a love for writing. By profession, some of them are college professors, some literary editors, some directors of literary institutions, some freelance writers and some professional writers. From the individual styles of the authors and the art of their writings, readers can easily detect traces of the authors' own experiences in life, their interests, as well as their aesthetic values. Most of the works in this collection are still written in the realistic style that represents, in a painstakingly fashioned fictional world, the changes of the times in urban and rural life. Having grown up in a more open era, the younger writers have been spared the hardships experienced by their predecessors, and therefore seek greater freedom in their writing. Whatever category of writers they belong to, all of them have gained their rightful places in Chinese literary circles over the last forty years. Shanghai writers tend to favor urban narratives more than other genres of writing. Most of the works in this collection can be characterized as urban literature with Shanghai characteristics, but there are also exceptions.

Called the "Paris of the East," Shanghai was already an international metropolis in the 1920s and 30s. Being the center of China's economy, culture and literature at the time, it housed a majority of writers of importance in the history of modern Chinese literature. The list includes Lu Xun, Guo Moruo, Mao Dun and Ba Jin, who had all written and published prolifically in Shanghai. Now, with Shanghai re-emerging as a globalized metropolis, the Shanghai writers who have appeared on the literary scene in the last forty years all face new challenges and literary quests of the times. I am confident that some of the older writers will produce new masterpieces. As for the fledging new generation of writers, we naturally expect them to go far in their long writing careers ahead of them. In due course, we will also introduce those writers who did not make it into this collection.

Wang Jiren
Series Editor

Contents

No Sail on the Western Sea

Nobody can really say
When it was that
The West
Became a symbol
And a space
Between reality
And illusion
That nobody thought unusual.

I

Nowadays, when people tell a story they always like to borrow something that is said to be an ancient song, preferably a folksong. This is because in itself, a folksong contains certain characteristics of a hidden mood. It also offers more than one possibility of limitless expansion. This applies particularly to ancient folksongs.

Of course, you too can also use this kind of old song.

You must, at all costs, first avoid the tedious and long-winded. You can't say what people may already know. For example, why you came here to these uplands and how you rode on this Liberation brand truck with its huge canvas cover. You know quite definitely that for anybody, and this naturally includes you, this is a unique experience that can never be repeated. You may say that this is nothing at all, it is just a premise, a background to the whole event. Nobody can contradict you. It's just you, consequently you cannot be doubted. The good natured reader will forgive you and indulge you in the way that a child is indulged. As far as they are concerned there is no basic difference between your seriousness or your frivolity. Whatever it is, you are just telling a story; you strive for a result for your story in the same way that the storyteller, Mr. Liu Baorui's stories make people concentrate. Do you feel aggrieved?

To start with, you feel, like everybody when they first go to Ali, that your heart-rate has changed. This is not just because Ali is the only empty space left in the world, or just because of its fantastic historical relics. At first, you worry that your heart cannot stand the altitude. You try hard to conceal this obstacle presented by your own body and to preserve an air of relaxed confidence and eagerness. You know that you are already middle aged. You are 36. The reader may not know that you are married with a sweet little daughter that looks like her mother.

In the same way, you have no intention of telling the reader that, by origin, you are the son of a fisherman and that the first pictures you drew were drawn on the sand of a beach with a finger moistened with seawater. In those days you frequently came across situations like this: several people would, by chance, get on a boat, one of those large sampans that can take six fishermen; to start with the wind and waves would be stable, then the weather would change and the waves would start to toss and there would be the beginnings of a disastrous encounter. You have no intention of talking about this or of soliciting the friendly reader's sympathy with these hair-raising adventures, more importantly you no longer take pride in your poetic romanticism. You are not a poet, besides, you are long past the age of writing poetry.

You keep a diary in the same way that others talk and eat, it's the spreading inertia of your life or maybe the demands of existence, after all, you are an intellectual by birth.

Maybe you want to say that you are not the only one from an intellectual family. Yes, Lu Gao is a friend from the "intellectual youth" sent to the countryside. When you went to university (at the age of 30) the age at which one stands on one's own feet, Lu Gao had already passed the exam to be a research student. But what does that signify? You know he also keeps a diary.

You know from your diary that you left Lhasa a good 30 days ago; and that your truck has been calmly soaking for seven days in that very ordinary river. There's a considerable degree of chance to numbers and one shouldn't elaborate on any problems. However, you do remember a romantic novel that you read a long time ago. In it, the place where the immortals lived was called hilltop. The altitude here is 6,040 meters, a true hilltop both in name and reality. Just seven days on the hilltop and several thousand years of mankind. That's what it says in the book.

If you actually trace out your route on a map there are bound to be numerous readers who will share your hardships with you. Don't bother.

In fact, you were mentally prepared for everything early on. It was you that actively encouraged the taking of this route. When you heard that the national route marked in a thick red line on the map had been abandoned years ago, you secretly made up your mind to persuade Lu Gao, the group leader, to follow it whatever it took. At the time, you advanced more than one reason, for example that it lay in the valley between the Gangdise and the Himalayas; that you could see the marvelous scenery on the border; that geographically speaking it was a bit closer and you could save on fuel and so on and so forth. Producing this sort of nonsense on the spur of the moment requires a certain inspiration.

Consequently, it would not be doing you an injustice to say that the considerable difficulties of this journey are of your own making. Although you are not a brash youngster, there is an excess of romanticism. But the fact that you escaped calamity by the skin of your teeth is proof of your luck and good fortune. Isn't that what Lu Gao said about you?

Remember, don't spin tales of woe to others and that includes not showing them the scars on your stomach. In this way your story will have some elasticity. The listeners will either let their imaginations run riot or will dismiss it with a laugh. Why must you insist that people should believe every last word?

II

That's what he may say, but I want to emphasize that it's all true. Why can't I tell people to look at my scars? Do you mean to say that after we've suffered so much, it's all fiction?

In the beginning we all thought that this was a one-time normal accident. There are a lot of this sort of accident on a journey and none of us thought anything of it. Even the curses of the driver were exactly the same, but there was that little stream. I guess it was the bit downstream, we seemed never to leave it. Neither sluggish nor rapid and always crystal clear so that you could see the bottom. Now and then we left it and now and then climbed along its muddy banks. Now we've stopped, the accelerator roared, it just shuddered a few times and then wouldn't budge.

The three of us, myself, Little Bai and the driver were in the driving cab. The driver was called Dadra. Ashen faced, Dadra trod on the accelerator. The truck had stopped exactly in the middle of the river, at this point about 20 meters across.

"It's no good, it won't move. We'll have to spend the night here." Little Bai turned and sought my views with a look.

"Dadra, should we get out and move the rocks?"

"Best get out and put up the cover. I said it won't move."

"What about trying the jack?"

"No use. You'd better go and ask and see if there's an army base hereabouts."

Dadra was referring to a row of old buildings about a couple of kilometers away. The buildings had tin roofs and people were doing something in front of them. Lu Gao enquired through the canvas from the body of the truck and I passed on Dadra's views. Lu Gao was silent for a couple of minutes and then reluctantly said: "All right."

Little Bai and I rolled up our trouser legs and got down. That made no real sense, the water came up to our thighs and soaked our trousers up to just below the waistband. It was freezing. Both legs soon stiffened and for a long while I couldn't take a single step. Little Bai was much the same. We couldn't stand there in the icy water and I quickly waded to the bank with Little Bai close behind me.

The sunshine overhead was strong and we simply took off our trousers, wrung out the water, hung them over our arms and made our way towards the buildings clad in our underpants. I looked back and saw Lu Gao and the merchant on the truck putting up the canvas awning over the body of the truck as far as the cab. The last down was Migmar.

Our shoes were dripping wet and squelched at every step, quite a beautiful sound. I could see Little Bai's plump white thighs and a line round thin ankles like a wound, an inflamed red. I was wearing a pair of khaki army trousers and Little Bai a pair of nylon swimming trunks.

The buildings didn't appear far away but after walking for ten minutes the distance didn't seem to have decreased at all. I know the air here is rarified and that the excellent visibility causes mistakes in estimating distances. It's too high above sea-level here.

The sun was so strong that the skin of our legs itched and I started to scratch. As if infected, Little Bai scratched too. I was wearing glasses for short sight which changed color and served as sunglasses so that I didn't see the shape of the person in front of the building. Little Bai said with some alarm: "It's a woman."

"Should we put our trousers on?" he asked.

"Don't bother, sitting in wet trousers can make you ill."

"Let's not wear them then, it makes no difference to me."

In our haste, we had forgotten something. This was remote Tibet, there might not be anybody who understood Chinese and neither Little Bai nor I could speak Tibetan. Go back and call them? We had three Tibetan companions, we ought to call on one of them to help.

It was a Tibetan woman of about 30. She stopped what she was doing and gazed steadily at us. I could see that her gaze was focused on our lower bodies. It must have been our bare legs that made us look so curious. I greeted her in Tibetan.

"Acha—Sister!"

She turned away nervously and quickly went inside.

She obviously didn't understand Chinese. My clumsy greeting had frightened her. I conferred with Little Bai and we put on our wet trousers.

I stood in the doorway and called *"Acha!"* again. This time two of them emerged together. The younger girl was about 17.

The buildings had obviously once housed an army unit. The peeling grey walls still bore the faint traces of written characters.

"... NITED, ALERT, [——], ... IVELY"

The tin-roofed buildings were public buildings built by the state, very different from the flat-roofed Tibetan houses. It looked as if the army unit had pulled out long ago and that the two women had been living there for some time. There was pile upon pile of animal dung and a simple sheep pen. The interior had been so blackened by smoke that the original color of the walls was no longer visible. The harsh light outside added to the internal gloom.

The girl was hiding behind the woman. I couldn't make myself clear and just gestured towards the truck in the river. The women understood and nodded in reply. I didn't know how to proceed. Fortunately they agreed to accompany us back to the river where the truck was stuck.

When we reached the river bank I called to our four companions to get off. As a result, Dadra stayed in the cab looking apathetically at Lu Gao, and Migmar and the merchant waded through the water.

Through the questioning of Migmar and the merchant we learned that there had been a very small military outpost here, in the buildings the two women occupied. Later, the road had been re-routed and the outpost relocated. For a hundred kilometers round, apart from a few scattered herds people like them there was no sign of life. The nearest place was the county town of Burang, about two hundred kilometers away. The women said that there had been no vehicles for at least six months. The last vehicles through had been three trucks together and one had been stuck for three months. In the end it had been pulled out by a tank. The people in that truck had left in the other two trucks.

Lu Gao silently circled the truck, now and then bending down to feel the tyres. I thought he must have been very cold, his face was pale, possibly to do with lack of oxygen. When at last he straightened up and moved towards the bank I could see from his face that what Dadra had said was true.

We definitely couldn't get away.

III

It's very difficult to explain how the water here could contain minerals and be bitter.

It was the first time that any of them had realized that there were rivers of bitter mineral water. The river held the truck and the truck held goods, so they could only put up a simple awning on the bank. This was the large rainproof canvas tarpaulin from the truck.

The sun was clearly setting but the light was still good. They would have to hurry to unload everything they needed from the truck in time. Pressure cooker, bags of rice, water can, camping stove, sleeping bags, bowls and chopsticks. That was all that could be thought of at the moment. They had to hurry, otherwise when the sun went down, going backwards and forwards in the icy water would be unimaginable.

The awning was put up at the foot of a small hillock by the river bank in front of us. They hoped that it would be a shelter from the wind. Everybody had learned of the high winds here. The amount of work required for moving was not great but breathing at altitude was difficult and the slightest exertion had already made them feel that they couldn't cope. Little Bai had even pulled a thermometer (air temperature gauge) from his bundle and taken the water temperature. It was 3° Celsius.

Dadra was the first to lie down, staring silent and open-eyed at the roof of the awning. Lu Gao was also quiet and busily searched nearby for stones to weigh down the perimeter of the awning. The merchant took the water can to look for water. Migmar thought for a moment and then followed him. Yao Liang took a fishing net that he had brought with him and went fishing in a backwater not far off. Little Bai took everybody's wet trousers and laid them out on some dry stones to dry.

Yao Liang had a good catch. It was difficult to imagine the sheer number of fish there were here. Yao Liang's catch consisted of fish from the plateau that had heads like catfish but very short bodies, he thought that they were a variety of catfish. The large were never less than a foot and the small about the width of your palm. The heads were large with well-developed cheeks.

Once the net was in, it was full in a few minutes. Seven fresh live fish hanging from the net. Yao Liang's delight can be imagined. Little Bai cried out in astonishment from a distance. At that moment Lu Gao accidentally glimpsed the expression of deep gloom on Dadra's face.

Although Yao Liang had advocated taking this route, the final decision had rested with Lu Gao. Lu Gao had taken Dadra into account. At the time Dadra had just said: "I want to see Buddha at the holy lake of Manasarovar (Lake Mapam Yumco), but the northern route bypasses it." This had finally caused Lu Gao to decide on the southern route.

In Zhongba County they had warned them that the southern route was unsafe—bandits were active in the border area, mostly remnants of the rebel forces and members of the opposing border security force. Perhaps because it was a truckload of men, there was courage in abundance. So they took the southern route.

The fact that it was called a national route had made them all happy. Vehicle tracks were no longer visible and making out the road itself was difficult. It would not be long before drifting sand would obliterate this thick red line, leaving not a trace.

The truck often got stuck in sandpits and couldn't go forward or back out. They had to dismount and find stones, dig out the sand and if that didn't work use the jack to raise the rear axle. In the distance a moving cloud of dust came closer and closer. Little Bai was the first to call out in astonishment: "Look! Wild horses!"

Yao Liang mumbled: "So many!"

The merchant quietly said: "They're wild asses."

Migmar said that he had seen them at Twin Lakes. Twin Lakes was the uninhabited area of Northwest Tibet. Wild asses were rare animals and difficult to find.

Little Bai clambered on to the top of the cab with a type 53 rifle, loaded a round into the breech and put off the safety catch. Dadra scowled and bellowed: "What do you think you're doing? Taking life?"

Lu Gao interjected: "Let off a round to disperse them, fire over their heads."

Little Bai resentfully fired into the air in the direction of the asses, unexpectedly causing this herd of rare animals to increase their speed and encircle the truck. At the closest they were only ten or more meters away and the tossing of their light brown manes and the fringe of white fur beneath their bellies could be seen clearly. They stood quite tall, about the height of the North Tibet horse, light-footed and agile, they certainly appeared to be able to gallop fast. They were fascinating.

Migmar and Little Bai tried to get close to them. They quickly dashed off in alarm, but not far, and stopped at a distance of just over ten meters, pawing the ground and snorting.

That was the time that Lu Gao had first discovered Dadra, his face filled with enmity, watching Little Bai's every move.

Dadra was a Buddhist. He was only 21. Little Bai was also 21. The youngest was Migmar who was nearly 20.

Strictly speaking, in Lhasa, fishing was not regarded as taking life. There were stallholders in Lhasa who sold fish. Many Tibetan compatriots eat fish. However, Dadra had an ugly look on his face. Lu Gao felt that this was not a good omen. He kept a close eye on Dadra's mood thereafter. He was the leader.

Apart from Dadra, the remainder, Lu Gao, Little Bai and Yao Liang, were just wearing underpants. Meanwhile, not far off, the two Tibetan women were watching what Little Bai was doing. They now knew that the older woman was called Pedron, aged

23 and sister-in-law of the girl Dolker. Pedron's man, Choegyal was away herding.

Migmar and the merchant went to fetch water from a direction pointed out to them by Pedron. It was about an hour and a half later, when Yao Liang had gutted the fish and was waiting for fresh water that they finally made out the two figures with the water can in the far distance. In a place with rivers, where water should have been no problem, it was water that was the first big problem. With all the jolting and bumping, a can of water lost half its water. In spite of taking turns to carry the can it was easy to see that they were exhausted. Yao Liang estimated that it was about 20 *li* (one *li* is 500 meters) there and back. Regrettably, the water container was plastic, holding only six liters, if it were six liters, then how much water was half? Six weary, dirty and hungry men! The women went back to cook. Time to go back and cook too. In an hour's time the sun will be setting.

IV

You are not too pleased with this journey to Ali.

You say that the site of the accident is too wild and that the snow-clad Himalayas to the south are too far away. There's no composition. For four artists, there could be nothing sadder than this. So you raise aestheticism's most airy-fairy topics: Romanticism and Imagination.

Your state of mind before coming to Ali very much resembled your state of mind before coming to Tibet. Full of every variety of great composition. Temples, snow-clad mountains, eagles and falcons, vast areas of gigantic ruins and a land so beautiful that it seems a construct of heaven. So many legends heard that the imagination naturally runs unbridled and cannot be reined in.

You were dissatisfied with life as an art lecturer in a normal college. So that when you received the letter from Lu Gao, you rather exceptionally lost sleep. You were envious and jealous of Lu

Gao going to Tibet. Lu Gao is a specialist creative member of the Artists' Association, the only art research student in Tibet. Why had you never thought of going to work in Tibet?

> Yao Liang: You know I'm in Tibet. I also know that you are thinking the same thing, you're having regrets. Don't ask me how I know, I just do. There's an opportunity. The Artists' Association is a member short and there's to be a big art exhibition in Tibet next year. The Association wants to transfer an art worker from the interior, no registration, for three years. Will you come? I think you will and so have written this letter. Reply to Lu Gao.

You don't say whether you replied to the letter or came straight away. Old friends and old colleagues all helped you prepare the exhibition. You waited in Chengdu for a fortnight before you got a plane ticket. The air stewardess told the passengers that Lhasa Gonggar Airport was below, and that greeny black flowing water was the Yarlong Tsangpo River. You discover that you are not at all as agitated or worried as you had originally thought you would be. Patiently, you look for the Potala Palace amidst all the greenery. Red palace walls! But it isn't. The passenger in the next seat tells you that it takes two and a half hours to get 95 kilometers from Lhasa. You calm down.

For no reason at all you remember a poem about Lhasa:

> In July it's all green
> And tomatoes are only
> One seventy a catty.

True, it's all green. It's now July, the white clouds are high in the sky and the green sea of barley in the river valley soothes your heart. The Potala is not greatly different from how you imagined it and the pavemented streets and the beautiful green shade makes you initially satisfied with Lhasa.

However, you discover that the whole of Lhasa, including the Potala, lacks ideal composition. Professional habits oppress you.

In the past, you had thought of it in terms that were too concrete. Lhasa had now become abstract, to be seen but not achieved. You begin to suspect your own perceptions and feelings. Then you attempt to reacquaint yourself with Lhasa from a different point of view. You hide up during the day and emerge at night and twist in and out of the maze of little alleys that surround the Barkhor. You also circle the Potala at a little distance seeking a transition. It's at that moment that you hear people talking of the marvels of Ali and you place limitless hope in its mysteries. You believe that Ali can restore you. You lack the ability to feel at ease in all circumstances nor are you properly aware of the true significance of the saying "be content with what you have."

"The All Tibet Art Exhibition" cannot do without Ali. The wall paintings in the ancient ruins may be the only ones that remain. The Artists' Association did not baulk at the cost and so forked out a sixth of its annual budget to hire this Liberation brand truck.

Estimated time, two months; estimated hire 5,500 yuan.

Little Bai is the art editor of a publishing company and so is Migmar. Migmar is a member of a branch of the Artists' Association with a reputation as legitimate as that of the truck. Little Bai is merely somebody from your home village who has come along for the ride and is paying his own travelling expenses. Little Bai has been in Tibet a little over six months, he was a friend from university in the year below you. You were very touched by the fact that Little Bai had sought leave of absence. He would meet his own travel expenses and receive no salary. The difference between you and Little Bai was that he had volunteered to move his registration and work in Tibet for eight years.

You could say that he was only 21. His youth is capital beyond value. Perhaps, if you were to be asked why you say this, your face would redden. You, Yao Liang, you have nothing to hide.

Leave a way out. What more is to be said?

Even to yourself, you dare not deny that you like Little Bai. You just dislike his myopic tortoiseshell glasses and his blindingly white bare legs. He really does not look like a male. But his enthusiasm pleases you and somewhere in there you detect the Yao Liang of ten years ago. Recollection makes you uncertain of yourself and you therefore decide to abandon recollection.

Will you abandon hope too? And imagination?

You are an artist. You should be ashamed of yourself. Since the truck got stuck you have only made two sketches. Two! In seven days!

The pots and pans, bowls and ladles under the awning, that was one, three of them went out and three of you stayed. Apart from cooking, what did you do day after day?

V

Yes, what did I do for those seven days?

Let's look at the diary.

The diary's too simple. Just a few sentences here and there.

19 September

It took a long time to get the engine started this morning, Dadra said the engine oil was frozen, as a result we used a blow torch for half an hour before the problem was solved. We spent the night on the truck. It was extremely cold and we all huddled together—apart from Dadra that is, he slept in the cabin. We formally set out at 9:15 a.m. Beijing time, we got stuck at about 4 p.m. and had to stop. There's no water for cooking here (fresh water), you have to fetch it from about 10 *li* away.

I caught some fish with a net. We had fish soup for supper, but Dadra did not eat a single mouthful. Lu Gao later warned me that Dadra had been angered by the fishing. Choegyal came over after nightfall and asked whether we wanted to stay in the building, it would only be two yuan a night each. We thought that the truck would have to be guarded. There were the merchant's goods to the value of four or five thousand yuan on board. We politely declined. Choegyal did not seem too happy. Pedron and Dolker did not come.

It's worth talking a little about Choegyal.

To start with, it was overcast that night. Then, later, there was a fierce rainstorm that lasted for several minutes. The depression in which were camped was like the pit of a leaking gutter. Fortunately we had not spread out our sleeping bags and so they didn't get wet. We hastily moved camp and put up the awning on the top of the hillock. We just had to put up with the wind. The sky cleared after the rain and was filled with beautiful stars. This was when Choegyal came over. It was our headlights that served as his signpost. He didn't speak a word of Chinese; outwardly he appears a typical burly fellow, his ruggedness clearly apparent.

Migmar talked to him and translated into Chinese where necessary. He said he was Pedron's man. He said he welcomed us to his house where it was warm. He said it would only be two yuan a night each. He said he was a herdsman from Kham and that he had been here for over two years. He said his name was Choegyal.

I guessed that he was about 28. He seemed a little younger compared with Pedron. Pedron was only 23 but you would not have thought it.

Following discussion, Lu Gao decided not to stay with Choegyal's family. Under the bright lamplight we could clearly see the sudden look of displeasure on Choegyal's face. True, 12 yuan a night was no small income. At this point I noticed an expression of cunning on his face that did not at all match his outward appearance and which passed in a flash. Little Bai quickly exchanged a glance with me and I knew that he had noticed it too. In the days to come Choegyal's family were to form an unbreakable link with us.

Before going to sleep that night we encountered another problem. The howling of wolves. Before it got dark two wolves had been quietly observing us from a distance of about 200 meters. They were clearly a male and his mate. The howling started as soon as darkness fell. Quite like the wailing of a baby, not too detestable and in fact rather pitiable. I tried hard to envisage a terrible outcome but there was none. However they were quite obviously close in the darkness. Little Bai was nervous and could not take his attention off the howling. One moment he would concentrate on it and the next pretend that he wasn't concerned at all. He asked me whether I had read Jack London's novels. I had read them all, including those that hadn't been translated. He looked disappointed. He clearly believed that other people could not understand the gravity of the current situation; people who had read Jack London would feel very differently. I was not in the least disturbed, this was incomprehensible. I am not a particularly brave man. Lu Gao's quiet level tone was obviously a great comfort to Little Bai. "They're not hungry. The howling of hungry wolves would terrify you. They're just passing the time, as we do, by singing."

Little Bai had already heard Yao Liang's stories of Lu Gao hunting. For Little Bai hunting was a great excitement and there were wild animals within sight here. Moreover they had arms and ammunition as well as the great hunter Lu Gao.

"Still the same pair of wolves?"

"Maybe it's another couple. That pair couldn't stand guard as long as this. Wolves are not that patient."

"Alaskan wolves have more patience than people."

"You mean the wolf in *Love of the Wild*. London didn't know much about wolves even though he wrote about them several times."

Dadra's idea played a decisive role.

"We don't have the kindling or wood for a fire and we couldn't stand keeping the fire in all night. I think we should light a blow torch on low flame, no pumping. The wolves won't dare to come close. It's what we used to do in the wild."

I nudged Lu Gao and in a low voice warned: "Petrol."

Lu Gao asked Dadra how much fuel it would use overnight. Dadra said half a tin until dawn when the wolves would go. That's what we'll do.

Everybody went to sleep. I closed my eyes but didn't feel sleepy. The howling of the wolves rose and fell in waves and mingled with the snores of my companions to form a lullaby. Just as I was drowsing off, I was alerted by an unusual noise.

It was Little Bai next to me carefully grasping the rifle. I then clearly heard the sound of clinking metal from the direction of the stationary truck. I pulled at Little Bai, we helped each other up and crept towards the truck. There was a sound of water.

Little Bai fiercely opened and closed the rifle bolt, shouting: "Who's there?"

Somebody replied immediately and waded fearfully towards us. When he was close, we saw that it was the herdsman, Choegyal.

VI

Yao Liang had thought early on that it could be Choegyal and had consequently not been in the least surprised. He made Little Bai lower the rifle and Choegyal gave him a strange look.

Yao Liang did not think to wonder why Choegyal had looked at him like that.

"Brother Yao, shall I go and wake Migmar? So he can question him!"

Yao Liang thought it over: "Never mind, let him go."

"Just let him go like that?"

"Even if we do, what then? Besides, what would we get out

of him? Do you suppose that he'd say anything?"

Little Bai snorted angrily and signaled to Choegyal to go back. Qiajia walked away in the direction of his home. Little Bai listened to the sound of his footsteps disappearing into the distance and then complained to Yao Liang: "Isn't it obvious, he came to steal."

"Not so loud. He may not be far off."

"You kept your voice down just now, you're afraid of something. He can't understand Chinese anyhow."

After a few steps, Yao Liang thought of something: "Don't mention this tomorrow, especially not to our Tibetan comrades."

"Why? I don't understand what you're frightened of."

"It's not that. I don't want to cause any misunderstanding."

"What is there to misunderstand? Isn't it a fact that Choegyal was on our truck in the middle of the night? We don't say that he was up to something but he was there, how can that not be said?"

"This is a nationalities area. We'll find an opportunity to talk to Lu Gao on our own tomorrow, the three of us should discuss it first."

As they went to bed again, Little Bai quietly nudged Yao Liang: "Do you think he'll be back?"

"No, he knows we're prepared."

"Then I'll sleep easily, until dawn."

Within ten minutes Little Bai had started snoring. Yao Liang laughed to himself and prepared to sleep. The howling of the wolves was exceptionally clear, the only sound that filled the whole of space.

The sun shone uncomfortably in Yao Liang's eyes and he woke. Only the merchant's sleeping bag was empty, the others were still asleep. Yao Liang tried hard not to make any noise as he got up. He thought that it was probably all right to wash in bitter water. Everyone had been in the water the previous day and there had been no abnormal reaction on their arms and legs. He took his washing things and made for the river bank alone.

The merchant was in the body of the truck probably attending to his goods.

"Old Yao, the water's risen, it's almost at the floor of the truck. Do you think my stuff will get wet?"

"Have you got anything that's especially likely to be damaged by water? Medicines or anything else precious?"

The water had clearly risen considerably. When he stooped to rinse out his mouth he could see that barely half a foot remained between the water and the floor of the truck. Although the morning sunshine was on its way the temperature was still low. He hesitated a moment and then took off his trousers and waded out to the truck to help the merchant re-arrange his goods.

"Aiya! It's so cold. It would have taken a long time by myself."

"Not at all, I was already here."

"I'm putting you to a lot of trouble."

As far as possible they hung the lighter packages from the frame for the canvas cover and piled the heavier ones up to avoid the water if it rose further and soaked the body of the truck. By the time that they had finished to their satisfaction the other four were up and washing.

"Little Bai, let's you and I go and fetch water."

"Right."

"Old Yao, you stay and cook. I'll go with Little Bai."

"It's better if I go, you need to think about what we're going to do, we can't just wait here forever."

The merchant said little, picked up the water can and pulled at Little Bai. "We'll go. Old Yao is cooking and Old Lu will be discussing with everybody to get ideas. I've been once and know the way."

"Migmar, take a look round and see if there's anything that can be burnt as firewood. We can't always be burning oil."

Dadra was buried in sleep, though the sun was already very high.

Lu Gao and Yao Liang remained behind to do the cooking.

In passing, Yao Liang mentioned the business with Choegyal the night before. The result of their discussion was that they should all take turns in standing guard at night. Standing didn't actually mean standing up, it would be enough to lie awake in a sleeping bag. Two hours at a time. Everybody had an absolute duty to guard the truck.

"But, Lu Gao what are we going to do? Wait for a vehicle to arrive? Didn't Pedron say yesterday that there hadn't been a vehicle through here for six months?"

"It's no good just dumbly waiting here. Wait until Dadra's up and we'll all talk it through together. See what people have to say. In this sort of situation drivers often have a solution."

"But Dadra …"

"Let it be. Don't argue with him. All drivers are bad tempered but when they're really up against it, their heart's in the right place."

"There's still petrol but we don't have much reserve fuel. If we go on cooking three meals a day and burning a light all night, I'm afraid it'll all be soon gone. We're 200 kilometers from Burang. Who knows how long we could be trapped here? Didn't Pedron say that the last truck was stuck for a full three months? If we're lucky and do get rescued, where are we going to get all those liters of fuel? Passing trucks are all long distance, nobody has surplus fuel. Without fuel, the truck's just a pile of junk even if we do pull it out."

"I'm thinking of the food. We've only a few dozen kilos of rice and with six people it'll be gone in two or three days. What do we do then? I shouldn't think Choegyal's family will have much grain they can sell us …"

Take no thought for the future and there will be sorrow in the present. Both had now arisen. Yao Liang thought first of fish. Fish were a partial solution of the food problem. Straight away there was another problem, salt. They had a small packet of pure salt, about 50 grams, enough to keep them going for a short while but a problem for any longer. As for hunting, that had just been an idea which he hadn't raised with Lu Gao. After Dadra had lost his temper with Little Bai, Lu Gao had seriously proposed a ban on hunting (privately of course, to Yao Liang and Little Bai). Yao Liang thought to himself, if there was really nothing to eat, then they'd bloody well hunt without Dadra knowing. There were gazelle, roebuck and wild asses aplenty. If there was nothing to eat they couldn't just starve to death in veneration of Buddha. Besides, since Buddhism was merciful, how could old man Buddha allow it? They had more than 300 rounds of ammunition.

Migmar was the first back with good news. There was "crawling pine" here, a kind of dwarf high plateau plant with a developed root system, almost ideal as firewood. There were also (heaven fails not man) mushrooms!

VII

You may not have the time to talk about Guge. Indeed, you may find it embarrassing to talk about it. Guge was a tune of another sort. After so many disasters, have you lost faith in Guge? After all, no matter what, you did several paintings there.

Zanda is a small county town of no great reputation. You say that you will never forget Ouyang, the county head. You said that you would develop the souvenir photos that you had taken and return them quickly. Without his help the outcome would have been difficult to imagine.

First it was petrol, you had petrol coupons, valid for the whole autonomous region. But local policy was clear, cash only. You and Migmar negotiated back and forth but the official at the petrol depot just slammed the shutter in your face. Your official funds were limited and the money people had on them was insignificant. The official price of petrol in Lhasa was a little over 0.7 yuan a liter. In Zanda the negotiated price at the petrol depot was two yuan a liter! When you left Burang you could see the bottom of the tank. To say nothing of returning, even the journey there and back to the ruins of Guge in Zanda County was beyond contemplation.

You could only stopover. There were rooms at the county guest house but nobody to cook. If you stayed, you had to do your own cooking. Not a soul was at home when you went looking for the county leadership.

Stuck for several days, people got wise, stopped complaining and resigned themselves to fate. Adaptability to circumstance should be the most treasured experience of those who suffer calamity. You had bought rice and salt in Burang and two huge radishes.

To economize, meals were reduced by half, so that one radish would last two days (at two meals a day). Not many tins were left and you no longer dared open them thoughtlessly. You were all bored to death during the day and were shut indoors doing you knew not what. Dadra and Migmar went out in search of a teahouse that served sugared tea. They were back an hour later, cursing that the *chang* (Tibetan barley alcohol) had been watered and that the sugared tea had been terribly expensive. Everybody was in a bad mood and nobody answered Dadra. Dadra was embarrassed, swore for a while, pulled up his duvet and slept, only waking for meals.

Lu Gao sketched his reconstructed impressions of the journey from memory and jotted down his recollections and feelings in the margins of the sketch. You simply searched out your sketchbook and produced a few according to a set pattern. During the journey, there were often extraordinary sights that took your breath away. Great billowing white clouds pressing upon the snow covered peaks on the horizon, the peaks themselves disappearing into the clouds with the sky above so transparent that it was unreal. A huge yak charging three gaunt wolves, the dust beneath its hooves making it look like a galloping cloud— and much, much more. This was when you asked Dadra to stop, his reactions always seemed exceptionally slow, seven or eight minutes later he would slowly depress the brake pedal and then innocently ask: "What did you say?"

"Go on. I didn't say anything. Keep going."

Lu Gao had brought a camera but it was of almost no use. Just a few lifeless snaps of inanimate objects taken at stops or in overnight lodgings. Lu Gao was incredibly patient throughout the journey and never showed any reaction to Dadra's lack of co-operation.

Little Bai still had the two books which never left his side. He must definitely have read them at least ten times. You ask him if he's still thinking of Princess. He doesn't even pretend to be angry as he used to and pays you no attention. But he clearly heard what you asked. This sort of situation continues day after day. At lunchtime, somebody knocks on the door. Ouyang, the county head has arrived. He'd just got back from his subordinate units, hadn't eaten and had come as soon as he heard. He was 51 and appeared completely Tibetan.

You set out your difficulties frankly. Petrol and food.

"Food's easy, come and eat with me. Umm, petrol, well, petrol, what about—how much ready cash can you produce?" Even county head Ouyang is at a loss. This causes you great disappointment.

Lu Gao tells him that you have hardly any money to buy petrol. There is very little left over from the money you had for food and lodging on the journey. How many liters of petrol would 20 or 30 yuan buy?

You thought that he would have a cook to prepare meals and that it would be rather special and that your food would improve. You realized your mistake when you arrived. It was a small room of seven square meters into which a bed and a three drawer desk had been crammed. It was both bedroom and office.

"One cook is on holiday and the other is ill in Lhasa. Everybody's been cooking for themselves for six months. So I'll be your cook for the next few days, I'm not too bad at it."

Ouyang was from Jiangjin County in eastern Sichuan. He had been a "little devil," a bugler with the 18th Army when it entered Tibet in 1950. He changed trades and stayed in Tibet.

"My wife was transferred back home, she was the only typist

in the county. She was ill and the child wasn't well either. He's a boy, he got into a fight when he was young and lost an eye, he can't see. Would you like bamboo shoots? They're dried, from Anhui."

There was nothing else to eat, cauliflower or dried bean curd or anything else to give you.

"Sometimes we get vegetables from Xinjiang but they are more or less rotten by the time they get here. They come from Kashgar via Rutog. It takes a long time by truck from Lhasa and it's not worthwhile, the loss is too great and it's too expensive. A catty of cabbage is one yuan sixty and tomatoes five yuan. Fish is cheap here, cheaper than Lhasa. I hear the fish in Lhasa is the cheapest in the whole country. Do you eat fish? I'll try and get some fish for you."

You asked him about his views on internal transfers. He told you that it was not like Lhasa here, nor like several other areas. There was a shortage of cadres, generally there was even a serious shortage of working personnel who knew just a few characters, not to mention county level cadres with some ability. He said that he had a digestive illness which he suspected was stomach cancer, however, he hadn't mentioned it to the county committee. He had thought of an internal transfer but not terribly hard. Another three to five years, it would be the same anywhere. He knew this area well and was accustomed to it. It would take anybody else a very long time to get to know it well. Just a few more years until he retired (here, he sighed gently: if he lived that long) and then go back together and enjoy a few years of ease. Plant vegetables and raise a few chickens and ducks. He had a younger brother with a large family who'd had a grandson the year before last.

There was a feeling in your heart that you could not express. You went outside by yourself and walked a long way until Little Bai found you and called you back to eat. Early next day you went to Guge.

The petrol problem was finally solved by exchanging your coupons at the county committee for 100 liters worth of car petrol coupons. You then gave county head Ouyang this 100 liters worth of car coupons which, if the car didn't visit Xigaze or Lhasa, would expire after the New Year. Cars seldom left Ali and thus the county head's car had no fuel and he had to make his rural visits on horseback. Lu Gao burst into tears when he was given the 100 liters worth of coupons. This was the first time that you had seen Lu Gao weep and you had known each other for 16 years. Ouyang then came to an arrangement with the petrol depot whereby they sold you 100 liters of petrol at the reduced cash price of 2.30 yuan a liter. It was doubtful whether you would have been able to return to Lhasa without the help of county head Ouyang.

There was no way that you could express your gratitude until Lu Gao had the idea that you should take some photographs of Ouyang, particularly some in color. The first thing you would do when you returned to Lhasa would be to develop the black and white prints and send them to him (color film had to go back to the interior for developing). This gave you some comfort.

VIII

When I saw the mushrooms I really thought I was hallucinating. Real fleshy grey mushrooms, of the sort that grow profusely in the hill districts of my home province in the North East. They are delicious with meat, in soup, and with chicken stew.

Migmar had returned with four mushrooms, enough to make a fresh mushroom soup. I couldn't bear to eat them at once but kept them for supper and put them under the awning in the shade. We still had some tinned food. Meat and fresh mushroom soup. Thinking about it increased my appetite and made my mouth water.

I used a little water left over from the previous day to make a thick gruel and added a tin of pickled Sichuan vegetables and pork strips. We woke up Dadra to wash, waited for Little Bai and the merchant to return and all eat together.

While we were eating, Lu Gao asked for everybody's ideas on what our next step should be.

I sounded out Dadra on whether or not we might manage without getting another vehicle to tow us out, perhaps there was some hope?

Dadra seemed disinclined to say anything and just snorted.

Little Bai and Migmar suggested that we should send somebody to find a vehicle that would rescue us.

"Since we can't save ourselves, we must make good use of the time to go and look for somebody, being stuck here is not an option. I'll go," said Little Bai.

The merchant interjected: "No. You couldn't cope with the short distance when we went to fetch water just now. It's 200 kilometers to Burang."

"Well, what do we do, just sit here and wait to die?"

"Don't be so gloomy, Little Bai." Lu Gao turned to the merchant: "Somebody will have to go, but Little Bai is not fit enough. I wonder if this is the way to do it—you, Migmar and I, the three of us go together. Dadra guards the truck, Old Yao does the cooking and Little Bai helps with odd jobs, what do you say?"

I said: "I should go with them, you need to stay here in overall command, you're the leader."

"You won't do, you've always had a heart problem, you won't be able to manage such a long journey, you'll be a burden if you fall ill. You needn't think that staying will be any easier. It will be several days here, possibly longer, there could be all sorts of unforeseen difficulties."

Dadra finally spoke up: "Old Lu, it's better if I go and you stay. First of all we Tibetans are fitter; next I'm a driver and it's easier for me to find a vehicle. There are very few Han comrades here, all drivers are Tibetan and you won't be able to communicate with them because of language difficulties. You three stay. I'll go, I need to find *chang* and sugared tea to drink, I've been stifled these last few days."

He smiled as he spoke. I discovered for the first time that

he was attractive when he smiled, attractive and very young, he was only 21.

It was decided. Once decided there was no hesitation, finish eating and then leave. I suddenly thought of those four mushrooms.

"Wait a moment, wait and eat a bit more."

I cooked the mushrooms with a tin of steamed pork, it's fragrance filled the air. Everybody applauded and were lavish in their praise. I was inwardly proud of that soup. On this journey I was the cook and alternate manager. I packed them half the tins and food for their journey.

"No, we don't want it. We needn't take so much," said Migmar.

Dadra said: "We'll be all right when reach somewhere where there are people, we'll get *tsamba* (a Tibetan staple foodstuff) and tea to drink. We won't starve to death in a Tibetan area."

The merchant said that they could buy food once they'd left, they only need take enough food for a day. I said that it was a long journey and they would be physically exhausted, they must take enough food with them. Those that stayed behind would manage, we could pick mushrooms and go fishing. The result was a compromise. Migmar and Dadra seemed in a good mood but the merchant, who was older and more thoughtful, didn't appear so optimistic. However, you could see that he was suppressing his own feelings so as not to influence his two young companions.

Just before they left, the merchant took me aside.

"Old Yao, I'm entrusting the goods on the truck to you. You're a friend that can be relied on. I know about Choegyal coming last night and I thank you. When I got up this morning I was anxious to go and check the goods, there was nothing missing. Could I trouble you further over the next few days?"

"Don't worry. We'll look after it. Set your mind at rest."

They left.

It's odd when you think of it. They were off to get help but I was utterly miserable. As I watched the outline of those three figures gradually disappearing into the distance I wept tears of final separation, as if seeing a close relative off to war. I covertly glanced at the other two; Little Bai was as moved as I was; Lu Gao rarely showed his feelings and more than once had called me emotional.

Life for the three of us that were left had to adopt a different rhythm.

Lu Gao and I went looking for firewood and mushrooms. Little Bai was exhausted from the 20 *li* journey to fetch water. We made him lie down.

The climate here is unusual. It changes just like that. Lu Gao and I had not gone far when a cloud appeared in the clear sky and when it was overhead the rain came bucketing down. I had no protection from the rain and shared an old sack over our heads; as a result, both of us were completely soaked through. It only rained for seven or eight minutes and then the sky turned a brilliant blue, just leaving the sandy gravel a darker shade. We were happily drenched and struck up a song that we had known when we were young:

> On the side of the fast flowing river
> Sitting on a steep little bank
> I see sweet home
> With its pastures green.

"I say boss, can we go hunting now?"

"You can't hunt wild asses or roebuck."

"Aren't the roebuck here called *she,* musk deer?"

"They are. They're all precious animals, what's strange is that there should be so many here. Nobody at home would believe you."

"No hunting wild asses and roebuck then."

"There's not much food. They're going to Burang, at least a fortnight there and back. A fortnight!"

"Well, more or less ten days. If you think, it'll take six or seven days to walk there, three days for finding a vehicle and driving back will be enough. They won't dawdle."

"But there's not even five kilos of rice left."

"That's why I said we should go hunting. The task of hunting is yours and Little Bai's. He's desperate to go hunting."

We were out for several hours with little return, two roots of crawling pine and three mushrooms. Little Bai was still asleep when we returned. Beside his pillow was a profusely illustrated book, the *Philosophy of Art* by the Frenchman, Hippolyte Taine.

We didn't wake him. Lu Gao chopped up the firewood with a vegetable cleaver and I rinsed the rice in river water. At two ounces of rice each I'd probably used six ounces, we couldn't go on happily eating cooked rice at this rate.

Lu Gao went fishing. We were both wearing underpants, our wet clothing was spread out on the awning to dry. He was better at fishing than I, a natural expert.

I was busy at the stove when Little Bai somehow woke up and took me by surprise by saying quietly behind me: "How I slept, I must have been tired, where's Teacher Lu?"

"He's gone fishing."

"Really? I'll go and see!"

He rushed off. Had he known that Lu Gao would be taking him hunting in the next few days, he would have been delirious with joy.

Some of the firewood was green and produced smoke rather than flame. I blew at it until my eyes were red. My backside stuck out. I blew away in this position with my eyes closed, hoping that they would be more comfortable this way. When I opened my eyes again, I caught sight, between my bare legs, of Pedron and Dolker.

I blushed.

IX

Despite his masculinity, Yao Liang was deeply embarrassed by his predicament. Bending over bare chested and in his underpants, to have caught sight of two young women between his legs as it were, was beyond funny. Should he extricate himself by laughing?

The two women were laughing uncontrollably. The situation caused them boundless amusement. Yao Liang didn't know how to put an end to it all. Should he straighten up and greet them? That would be a bit too ... well ... He decided to continue blowing. He pretended that he hadn't seen them. Then, during the process of blowing, carefully and under control, he lowered his rump. He made an effort to appear relaxed and untroubled and finally ended in a squatting position. At this point he experienced a feeling of relaxation difficult to describe in words. He decided to turn round, he was very calm.

No need to turn round, he felt that they had already come up behind him. He merely had to turn sideways to greet them.

Relaxation lent him inspiration, he realized that he should pour a little petrol on the green wood. Then he wouldn't need to blow the fire with his backside in the air.

They watched curiously as he washed the mushrooms and tore them into strips and then emptied the remaining half tin of steamed pork into the soup to cook. When he put the mushroom strips into the pot they both let go an involuntary exclamation. By now, Yao Liang had long forgotten that he was half-naked and was proud of the fact that there were spectators observing his cooking.

Lu Gao and Little Bai returned with 20 or 30 river fish strung on a wire. This also excited the amazement of the two women. The fish had already been gutted and could go straight into the pot.

Lu Gao and Yao Liang were both half-naked. Little Bai was a little more elegantly dressed in a white shirt (his nether regions clad in close-fitting swimming trunks). The women broke into smiles. They nodded good naturedly to them and the women returned their nods in a seemingly mechanical reaction. Their attention was still on Little Bai's legs.

They had brought several tins of lard with them, there would seem to be no problem over fat in the short term. There were now two women guests. Yao Liang decided to cook roast fish. There was no common language and no way to converse but, of their own accord, the women capably helped Yao Liang tend the fire. They were obviously excited by the fragrant smell of the frying fish and Dolker simply stood by the fish pan watching the fresh fish as it turned yellow in the oil, her mouth openly watering. She presented the very image of a greedy child.

"Old Lu, ask them to stay and eat?"

"Of course. Dolker's quite attractive."

There was no scallion, ginger or garlic but the seasoning was complete enough. It was a sumptuous picnic, but how could one invite them to sit and eat. First point to the dish and then point at the ground? No good. When Little Bai gestured to his mouth with both hands little Dolker vigorously waved a hand in refusal and shyly hid behind Pedron. Then Yao Liang had an idea, he filled a bowl of mushroom soup for himself, Lu Gao and Little Bai which they then started to eat with every appearance of enjoying the delicious taste. This caused Pedron and Dolker to unconsciously open their mouths slightly. Yao Liang then used an enamel spoon to fill them a bowl each. Dolker looked at Pedron and didn't dip her spoon in the bowl until she had seen Pedron slowly swallow a mouthful of mushrooms.

The three of them looked on and smiled at each other.

The two women smiled as they eat. No one knew whether this was out of enjoyment of the delicious mushrooms or the need to respond to the good intentions of the host with a smiling countenance. By now, Little Bai and Yao Liang had forgotten the unpleasantness of the previous night and that Pedron was Choegyal's wife and Dolker his younger sister.

Dolker finished eating first. Yao Liang reached over, took her bowl and re-filled it. She nodded happily and handed him the bowl without a trace of bashfulness. This small gesture made her appear very attractive. Yao Liang noted her rosy complexion and regular white teeth.

"Dolker's so good-looking, she's our Princess."

From this moment on, Dolker's name was replaced by that of *gong zhu*—Princess.

The two women happily eat the mushrooms and finished off the remaining mushroom soup. However, when it came to eating the fish, however much they attempted to stimulate their appetites by chewing and swallowing, they both firmly refused. Lu Gao said that it was not long since Tibetan comrades in Lhasa had started to eat fish, the lower levels still couldn't accept this sort of contemporary "civilization," they shouldn't force it. To go to the extent of cooking and eating a sacred fish was a heinous crime.

Nobody noticed when it was that Little Bai had brought out his sketchbook. He rapidly made an accurate line sketch of Princess. He gave it to her, she was astonished. Pedron opened her eyes wide, pointed to Dolker and asked with a look: "Is it her?"

Little Bai nodded affirmatively. Princess looked feelingly at Little Bai for a time, chewed her lower lip and then solemnly bowed to him. Yao Liang laughed until the tears came. Lu Gao told Little Bai to give her the sketch. Little Bai tore it out and she made another deeply felt bow to Little Bai as she took it. The sun was beginning to go down, Pedron pulled at Princess as if suddenly remembering something, the two of them hurriedly motioned to their hosts and left in the direction of home.

They left, and seemed to have taken the atmosphere with them. In front of the awning it was suddenly silent. Nobody spoke for a very long time, nobody took any notice of anybody else and nobody did anything. Later, probably because it was getting cold, Lu Gao reached down his clothes from the awning and dressed, Yao Liang and Little Bai also got dressed.

Little Bai took up the can and, without a word to either Yao or Lu made off in the direction of the water. Lu Gao looked at Yao Liang and then, head down and keeping his distance, neither slow nor fast tailed Little Bai as one after the other, they gradually disappeared behind the sand dunes.

In the final diary entry for that day, Yao Liang wrote:

"... there was nothing to do, so the three of us didn't feel liking chatting and went to bed while the sun was still above the horizon. The first on guard was Little Bai and then me, followed by Lu Gao. Little Bai has found another book to read, Boccaccio's *Decameron*. Lu Gao has closed his eyes, whether he is asleep or not, I don't know. I am writing the diary. The sun has descended to the horizon, turned red and no longer dazzles the eyes. A full circle, three quarters, an exact semi-circle, a quarter, bit by bit it has dissolved into an irregular red strip. The sand dunes and wasteland are stained with red. The scene fills me with an irrational fear. What kind of omen is this? No more fantasizing. I am scaring myself. Go to sleep, go to sleep."

X

You're very interesting. When other people visit Ali, they always talk in immense detail about Guge. Is Guge really that wonderful? In fact it's rather wonderful that you should say it's wonderful. But you didn't talk about Guge. Why do you want to keep back the story of Guge?

When you reach Zanda the ruins of Guge are a short distance away. It was during the discussion of Guge that you first heard of the Tholing Monastery.

Will you go? Of course you will. Ouyang, the county head says that the wall-paintings are famous. Since there are wall-paintings you must go, all the more so since they are famous. You think that this so-called fame probably means that they are comparatively well preserved in terms of the county. As if he can read your mind, Ouyang says: "I don't understand. Experts say that they are first rate at a national level."

Your longing for Guge is urgent and you decide to go on to the Tholing Monastery after you have come back from the ruins of the ancient kingdom of Guge. You clearly pay no attention to the non-expert words of Ouyang. Because of shortness of time or for other reasons you may have lost this opportunity of visiting the Tholing Monastery. Moreover you know very well that you and your companions Lu Gao and Little Bai will never visit Zanda again.

Fortunately, there is no shortage of time and there are no other reasons. Fortunately.

But in your gut you will regret this, regret it bitterly.

This is no exaggeration, it is something you said yourself.

You say that you were all exhausted when you got back from Guge. You lay flat out on the beds when you got to the reception center. Feet unwashed and disinclined to eat. You hadn't had a whole night's sleep for three days, not to mention such modern habits as taking off your shoes and washing your feet. Ouyang's communicator came over to ask after you and said that you were going over to eat shortly. Much against your will you crawled to your feet and washed your faces.

During the meal Ouyang asked when you were thinking of going to the Tholing Monastery. You nearly blurted out: "Leave it!" That was something for Lu Gao to say to Ouyang. Lu Gao said early tomorrow morning. He also said that he wanted to photograph the wall-paintings and hoped that county head Ouyang could be of assistance. Ouyang tells his communicator to heat some water so that you can wash your feet and go to bed early after you have bathed your feet. Perhaps you enter the land of dreams before it's dark. In your dreams you are still walking amongst the ruined walls and frescoes of Guge. You had soon forgotten the wretched Tholing Monastery.

The magnificent Tuolin wall paintings make an unforgettable impression on you. This was when you had just returned from the ruins of Guge and when you were gorged with the superb artistry of the surviving Guge frescoes! Moreover, you had no conception of the sheer scale of the Tholing Monastery. This temple, which clings to the side of a mountain, is a structure which dates from the 10th century, several decades earlier than the Potala. Once in the temple, you each made your own way independent of each other. You first circled round the four corners.

At each of the four corners there is a pagoda whose form opens your eyes to a new world. Your interest in architecture is no less than your interest in painting. Imposing architecture has often been an artistic and creative stimulus for you. Then you spent a long time making a sketch of the whole scene.

There were two lamas, one young, one old, living in rather a small building. You pushed the door open and went in, the old lama was reciting a sutra with closed eyes in front of a niche containing a small Buddha. The young lama was sweeping the ground outside. For fear of disturbing the lama, you quickly withdrew but noticed that there was a faint faded fresco on the wall in which the niche was set. Once outside again, you couldn't help raising a corner of the curtain and looking in. That's how it was.

After you had looked at the main wall paintings of the temple you were determined to explore the meaning of the frescoes in the small building. All the wall-paintings in the Tholing Monastery have been more or less preserved intact, but that was not the main point.

The frescoes here are polychromatic and because of their comparative early date are more common-or-garden and secular. In this respect they are different from other wall-paintings in Tibet. Wall-paintings elsewhere are almost all of religious subjects and in their form and use of color are closer to the style of the Buddhist wall paintings of the interior. It is not the same here. The pervading sentiment of the daily life of humanity makes the paintings of the Tholing Monastery closer to folk-art with numerous animal forms and a technique which clearly owes much to the style of the two Han dynasties and late Tang in its emphasis on spontaneity.

The frescoes inside this building was already badly faded. This was not the case with rest of the wall-paintings in the temple. You inwardly hoped that that it was from an earlier period, perhaps that it was a fresco of the only remaining building of a small temple which had existed before the Tholing Monastery had been built. In which case the wall-paintings in this building would be even more valuable.

You attempted to find Migmar and discuss your idea with him and get him to negotiate with the lama so that you could go and take a detailed look at the wall-paintings in the building. Migmar, dressed as he was in the modern style, talked a long time with the monk in the Lhasa dialect. Without uttering a sound the monk turned away. Migmar gestured to you and spread his hands helplessly. There was nothing that could be done.

You didn't leave. Intentionally or otherwise you recalled a parable from the Bible. The parable of the lost sheep. A man had a flock of a hundred sheep and one was lost. The shepherd then let the 99 sheep go in order to search for the one sheep. When found, this single lost sheep received the particular attention of the shepherd. Interesting, don't you think? If this little building appeared the same to people you would perhaps give it a glance and pass on. With such a lot to see, there is no need to pay too much attention to one thing, there's not sufficient time. Now it's not the same. You are willing to spend any amount of time on it, it has become a lost sheep. You absolutely must find it and pay particular attention to it. Maybe there are corners where there are paintings that you have not seen, but they are no longer important.

XI

There was a high wind during the night and later on, after a heavy shower the temperature plummeted. You woke Lu Gao after you came off guard but you were not sleepy. You closed your eyes. You knew from the sound that Lu Gao had got up and left the tent. Then you opened your eyes and discovered that Little Bai also had his eyes open.

"What's Teacher Lu doing?"

"Haven't you slept at all?"

"I wonder whether Choegyal will come back."

"Don't let your imagination run away with you."

"Look, Brother Yao, it's snowing."

The large snowflakes drifted down heavily. At some point the wind had dropped. The night was still, there was nothing apart from the sound of falling snow.

"The wolves aren't howling, they howled non-stop when it was raining. I really feel like getting up and giving them a couple of shots."

"Little Bai, Lu Gao will be taking you out hunting tomorrow."

"I've been thinking about it all the time. It's cleared up."

The snow suddenly stopped. The night sky shone with bright closely packed stars. You simply pumped up the lamp and borrowed Little Bai's *Philosophy of Art* to read. Little Bai read the *Decameron*.

You didn't know what Lu Gao was doing, he wasn't to be seen. It was bitterly cold and every few minutes you changed hands to hold the book and withdrew the frozen hand under the bedclothes to get warm.

"Brother Yao, are you asleep? I can't sleep. How many days do you think we'll have to wait? I have a sort of premonition that Dadra and the others won't get back. I don't know how I got the idea.

"Last month I arrived from Qinghai by truck. After the Mount Dangla there was a lot of snow. But it was the height of summer in Beijing and Xi'an. The driver was a retired soldier who told stories the whole journey. He had a comrade who died in July last year on his way to a sentry post in Kekexili (Hoh Xil) to deliver supplies. You know the Twin Lakes, that twisted uninhabited area in the north, the sentry post is more than three hundred kilometers to the northwest of the Twin Lakes. It's an observation post. He was driving a single truck and believed that as it was summer there would be no problem.

"It was an unmetalled road and apart from delivering supplies once every two months there were no vehicles on it. A hundred kilometers beyond the Twin Lakes and near the Kekexili range, it started to snow and the road was suddenly obscured, he didn't dare carry on for fear of being stuck in a swamp, losing his way or overturning into the ditch. The topography there is very complicated. He told his assistant to get down from the truck and walk forward to find the way while the truck slowly followed on behind. It snowed harder and harder and it was soon half a meter deep. They couldn't go on. They pulled fur greatcoats from underneath the seat cushions and huddled in the cab waiting for the snow to stop.

"It snowed on without cease. During the night they could stand the cold no longer and got out of the truck and walked round it stamping their feet. His assistant was a young Tibetan and physically strong. He suggested that he should look around and see if they could find a herdsman's shelter. The driver agreed. Neither of them wore padded cotton shoes. When the assistant left the driver gave him an old pair of tattered cotton gloves.

"It snowed for three and a half days. By midday of the third day, the assistant was frozen stiff and lost consciousness. Fortunately there was a herdsman at the place where he collapsed who discovered him when it stopped snowing and took him into the shelter. It was seven days before he regained consciousness and ten days before he remembered and could be carried on a stretcher back to the driver. The herdsman gathered others and they carried him back along the way he came for another two days. Brother Yao, it's snowing again, are you cold?

"When they got to the place where the truck had stopped, nobody said a word. The fuel tank was empty and there wasn't even any engine oil in the oil nozzle. The whole vehicle was burnt completely black and crumpled. The driver was frozen into a block of ice alongside, his hands and feet and the front of his coat burnt black. The snow round the remains of the truck had melted and then frozen. The snow was nearly a meter deep."

Outside, the snowflakes seemed unwilling to show any sign of weakness and fell thick and fast very quickly covering the ground in a thick layer. Lu Gao returned through the snow bearing the crawling pine that had been collected during the day.

"Wake up. Come on, sit up, light a bonfire and sing. Come on! What's up with you two?"

21 September

It snowed heavily last night to a depth of about seven inches. The sky cleared in the morning and we brushed away the snow in the front of the tent. In fact, this was much more than was necessary. By midday the snow had completely melted and soaked into the surface of the gravel and in the afternoon mist was rising from the ground all around. The snow seemed to have arrived as if by magic and to have disappeared as if by magic, not a trace of it remaining hidden on the ground. However, the story Little Bai had told during the night had its effect. The snow had fallen fiercely during the story. Lu Gao lit a bonfire in the snow and it should have been a cheerful summer night. Little Bai didn't speak again. I was in no mood for conversation. Our silence baffled Lu Gao. We all sat round the fire but nobody sang. It was a really long silent and dispiriting winter night.

In the morning—

XII

In the morning, it felt at once as if there had been some gain. There was no need to fetch water, there would be melted water from the snow.

Little Bai said that in books, if chickens drank melted snow they laid more eggs. Yao Liang said that village housewives would never let laying hens out after snowfall, they said that chickens would stop laying if they eat snow.

None of this was of any consequence. Having to walk 20 *li* fewer to fetch water was much more important than whether or not hens laid eggs. Lu Gao was cleaning the rifle and Little Bai discreetly moved in and spontaneously handed Lu Gao the components as well as polishing the stock with an oily rag.

When Lu Gao and Little Bai went out the snow had just begun to melt. Immediately after snowfall was a golden time for hunting—that was an iron rule.

The shoes of both were soon wet from walking in the snow. Little Bai was wearing low-waisted walking boots and Lu Gao leather shoes. This caused difficulties in walking. The sky was extraordinarily blue, the result of reflection from the snow. The first thing they met was a flock of large, low-flying birds. Little Bai was the first to call out.

"Look. Teacher Lu, birds, they're coming over!"

Lu Gao, the great hunter that Yao Liang had described was a real disappointment to Little Bai.

"Saw them."

"But why, why didn't you fire?"

"Did you see what kind of birds they were?"

"They seemed to be cranes."

"They're called black-necked cranes, they're a protected species."

The black-necked cranes were overhead, their wings beating in rhythm. Their long necks were a gleaming black.

"That's the first time that I've seen that kind of bird."

Lu Gao said: "Me too."

"How did you come to know they were black-necked cranes?"

"From books."

So that was it. So Lu Gao was like that too.

"Have you ever hunted?"

"No. I've never been outside Shenyang."

"Have you ever fired a gun? Target shooting?"

"Yes. I was quite good. Scored 47."

"Five rounds?"

"Ten rounds."

"You use it, I'm not used to a rifle."

"What gun did you use? I mean in the past."

"A shotgun."

"Double barreled?"

"It was."

"German made, of course?"

"Mmm."

"Where is it now?"

"I don't have it anymore. Isn't the sky blue!"

Little Bai discovered that there was something not quite right with Lu Gao's mood. He was changing the subject. There was something he was not revealing. People only discussed the weather when there was nothing to talk about. Pah! Weather.

"Teacher Lu, what have you ever shot?"

"Rabbits."

"And?"

"Pheasants."

"Foxes?"

"Yes."

"What about wolves?"

"Wolves are difficult to shoot."

So this was it. So—this—was—it!

"But your gun? How come it's gone?"

"I smashed it."

"Smashed it? How?"

Silence. Another flock of black-necked cranes flew over and on.

"Tell me about it."

The sun was out and the snow was melting rapidly. Fortunately the gravel surface was not muddy. Little Bai walked to the side and a little ahead of Lu Gao, looking at him with hopeful concentration.

How could Lu Gao be unaware of Little Bai's gaze? It was the morning after snow and despite the high latitude the sky was blue and so clear that it was almost transparent.

"There was a lad called Two Dog who went down to the country with us."

"I've heard Brother Yao talk about it. He also mentioned Lu Erh. He said Two Dog kicked Lu Erh and you beat up Two Dog. You swore at Two Dog and said he was just a dog. Brother Yao said Lu Erh was a dog, you looked on him as a younger brother."

"I throttled him."

"Brother Yao talked about that too. It was unbearable for him—when he talked about it his eyes reddened."

"Little Xiu, Two Dog's girl-friend, was seduced by the brigade accountant and threw herself down a well. Two Dog drank so much that he got stomach ulcers and nearly died. He went home half an invalid. I was disgusted, Little Xiu had been a classmate of mine at school."

"And later? What's this to do with the shotgun?"

"Later," said Lu Gao unwillingly.

"You took the gun and went to settle the score with the accountant?"

"I burnt down their stockpile of firewood. It's salt flats there and firewood is essential, there's no wood to burn on salt flats. His whole family depended on the woodpile that winter. And there were nine of them, they had a difficult time."

"They didn't find out who had done it?"

"They knew I'd done it but had no proof."

"They never took revenge on you?"

"He sought me out and said that in his heart he understood, said that because of this we should make friends. He said that next time Da Han was looking for work he could arrange for her to go home, from then on conditions would be more harmonious."

"Who's Da Han?"

"Everybody said she was my girl-friend, in fact she wasn't. She had done some washing for me. She was a fellow student and we arrived together."

"The accountant seems to have been very fair-minded."

"What?! Don't you forget Little Xiu! When I heard his businessman's tone of voice I was furious. I went back and sat alone by myself with the gun hanging above the *kang* bed-stove, gleaming in the light. I was moved to murder as I looked at it. If I decide to do something, I will always do it. I could think of nothing else. Killing him. Smashing his dog's face. My head was filled with these sort of ideas. Stuffed full. All because I saw the gun.

"If he hadn't spoken like that, if he had had a row with me, perhaps I might not have thought of killing him. All that night I polished the gun and made up cartridges. I put in double the normal amount of powder. I thought of how it would blast his face to a pulp. Later when I had polished the gun and loaded the cartridges into the breech I hung it on the wall and sat by the *kang* bed-stove in a daze. I thought of my mother and other relatives. And I thought of the man I wanted to kill. It was still dark. Everything would be concluded at dawn. I was waiting."

"But, Teacher Lu, you didn't think of the consequences."

"The speckled cock next door crowed once. It was always the first to crow. Today it's crowing would decide everything. I got up and took the gun from the wall and slowly walked outside. After the death of Lu Erh, the gun was my only friend."

"Isn't Brother Yao your best friend?"

"They're two different things. The gun was my life, I'd had it since I was a child. I was standing at the door and when the cock crowed for the second time I smashed the gun on a rock. It was not yet completely light. If it had been, perhaps it would have been too late."

"But ..." Little Bai probably wanted to say something, regret perhaps? In the end, he said nothing. Having heard this story perhaps, in his heart, Lu Gao was no longer such a hard man. Little Bai knew the axiom of the male: a man who was angry with himself was a good-for-nothing.

How easy it was to destroy one's own image! You only have to talk about some discreditable trifle and that is enough. Nobody will raise any doubts when you are talking about yourself.

The problem is, do you really want to destroy your own image?

Little Bai was not that simple. What had been Lu Gao's purpose in talking like that? Little Bai did not believe that Lu Gao was a useless male. However, Little Bai believed that the next time they went hunting it would be his, Little Bai's story.

XIII

Because it's Chapter XIII, this chapter is very short.

You asked county head Ouyang for his assistance. You just wanted to stay overnight at the temple and Ouyang arranged it. They all went back and you stayed behind by yourself sharing a room with a Tibetan from the department of religious affairs who had studied at a technical secondary school in the interior. He was now the administrator of the Tholing Monastery. You discussed your idea with him and he said that there was nothing that he could do. The old lama was the abbot of the monastery. Apart from the young monk (who was mute) he allowed nobody to enter the room. Eventually, he had an idea. He said that every evening at nightfall the lamas chanted the sutras in the main hall. It would be possible to take this opportunity to go and have a look. With luck the door might not be locked. Hopefully this would be the case. He also warned that chanting the sutras took about an hour and a half and that you should make good use of the time.

You arranged that he should wait outside the hall until the conclusion of the sutra chanting and warn you by whistling when it was over so that you could get out in time. It would depend upon your luck. You hadn't forgotten to bring your camera.

Your luck held, otherwise how could you have avoided catastrophe.

The door was not locked. You quickly went in. It was only then that you discovered that there were frescoes on three of the walls but that they had been badly smeared. Direct photography would be impossible. On the basis of form and content you

53

concluded that your original judgment had been correct, these frescoes were indeed dated earlier than those outside. They depicted some sky burials where the remnants of severed corpses were scattered left and right and where the faces of the heads were very lifelike. It was possible to see that the toes of the lower leg remnants had been powerfully represented.

What interested you most was a continuous scene that represented the process of change from ape to man. Starting with monkeys it gradually moved to half-monkey half-man, furred man and finally to man with his loins covered. Very redolent of the theory of evolution. The scene series was several hundreds of years before Darwin. You were simply amazed.

Photography was what was important now. You were concerned about color. The use of color in frescoes is of particular importance. Moreover unless the surface of the painting was cleaned to produce a clear image, the negative would be problematical and very possibly fuzzy.

There was no water, nor was there anything that could serve as a cloth. Time was pressing, you couldn't take everything into account and simply spat on the painting and rubbed it with your sleeve. Given the accumulated grime of years you rubbed for some time and could only clear a small patch. But the result excited you. The painting revealed its original appearance, its strong and yet pure colors in fresh contrast with each other. Rather like the color palette of Matisse—No! It was Matisse who so much resembled this.

Your enthusiasm increased to the point where you forgot that you had rubbed the sleeve of your jacket threadbare and had dried out your mouth of saliva. Most important of all you had forgotten the warning whistle. By the time that you were aware of somebody behind you, the old lama had been standing there for some time. You didn't know how to get out of the situation and just stood remorsefully in front of him with your head lowered.

"Go and get a bowl of water."

You had never imagined that he could speak Chinese.

Half a minute earlier you had been regretting that you had not photographed the portion of the painting that you had already cleaned in time. You had color film in your camera, Kodak, the world's number one roll film.

The result can be imagined. You and the old lama were busy into the night and cleaned all the paintings on the three walls. Using flash you photographed the whole and detail of all images. As you worked so you talked. Fifty years ago he had graduated from the Institute of Buddhism in Delhi; he had also taught Buddhism at a university in Beijing, that had been forty years ago. According to his analysis, the frescoes in this small room dated from the mid-Tang dynasty and pre-dated the introduction of Buddhism into Tibet. They were all that was left of a great achievement.

Your perseverance had reaped an unexpected reward and brought you an unforgettable Tibetan friend of vast learning. The old lama was seventy seven, before he left home to become a monk his name had been Byangchub Namgyai.

XIV

Little Bai was really a youngster. When he heard, after breakfast, that they were going hunting, his mood immediately lifted. He forgot what had happened the previous night, at his age, extremes of mood were unusual. I was in no good state of mind. I extravagantly used up all the available water when washing the bowls and refilled the can with melted snow water.

The sack of rice was sagging and there was not much salt left. We still had a few tins. Mostly pork. I had to find something to do otherwise I would have nothing to occupy my mind. I thought of drying the fish so that they would not go bad. I had decided that we would have baked fish for supper. Half-dried fish soaked in soya sauce with lard roasted over the flame would definitely taste good. If needs be, I could make a thin rice congee, three bowls for each of us.

Firewood was a problem. We had cleared the immediate locality of crawling pine and would have to go further afield to find any.

I saw them coming in the distance. I realized that I had been looking forward to seeing them since early morning. I watched them approach, Pedron was carefully carrying a greasy leather bag. Princess was gazing at our tent.

With a smile I made a gesture of welcome. With an expression of satisfaction, Pedron opened the bag and carefully extracted a number of large mushrooms. This was really more than I had expected. I clasped my hands and bowed in thanks. Princess seemed preoccupied and glanced hither and thither. I guessed she was looking for Little Bai.

Only Little Bai wore glasses. I made circles from finger and thumb and gestured over my eyes. Princess straight away nodded in confirmation. I then mimed the movements of shooting, but repeat as I might, she shook her head. I thought that she had probably never seen hunting with a gun, they were Buddhists who did not take life. Pedron gestured to me that she wanted Little Bai to do a portrait of her as well. I thought that as I had nothing to do I might as well do her a sketch.

The picture caught the look of Pedron. Although she could not be called pretty, her features were well defined and had the classic look of Khamba women. I made her sit by the tent and made several quick sketches from different angles.

Princess squatted behind me and watched motionless. Sometimes she shook her head in disagreement and sometimes a blank smile escaped her. I sketched on. There was the sound of a gunshot from the distance. And then another. Pedron's expression showed alarm and Princess was even more uneasy. I gestured to them that it was Little Bai out shooting but they still didn't understand. A serious sketch requires a great deal of time and this may have puzzled Pedron. She knew that the sketch that Little Bai had done the previous evening had almost been tossed off in a moment and she had been sitting here most of the day and I showed no sign of finishing, she couldn't bear it. She rushed over to see and looked attentively at the part round the eyes where the relationship between light and shade had been sketched out.

She then spoke to Princess in Tibetan. From the way in which Princess looked at her face and compared it with that in the picture, I thought that Pedron had asked her whether it was a good likeness. Princess seemed to have given a positive reply because Pedron happily returned to her original position with an expression of satisfaction.

I spent a long time adjusting her position with gestures to the point where it was basically restored to its original tranquil state. As I was dealing with the area either side of the tip of the nose I experienced an unusual feeling of joy, the subtle rise and fall, the melodic transition of grey between light and dark was beautiful beyond words. A sudden feeling swept over me and my heart was suddenly filled with tenderness.

No. The woman seated before me was coarse, her skin lacking texture. What I longed to touch was merely the woman in the picture. I had probably fallen in love with the person in the picture, otherwise why should I have felt tenderness or been moved?

In fact, things were a great deal simpler. I was in love with nobody, I was merely seeking release from a mental state rooted in fear. A sketch was just an uncompleted piece of work and those peculiar feelings only arose under peculiar circumstances. If I were to fall in love with anybody it would probably be with the exuberantly youthful Princess.

How did I not see that it was Little Bai who was the object of Princess's attention?

As I worked to complete the sketch my head mysteriously filled with strange ideas. I reminded myself that at times like these I should be thinking of my little daughter, my daughter— my daughter! For her sake I had no right to indulge in fantasy. I was a miserable Daoist whose sense of responsibility led me to shoulder all obligations. I was curious as to why it was that I had not warned myself, love—love and family?

I finished the sketch in little over an hour.

I liked this little draft. I felt that I had captured something that every artist strives for. I didn't even want to give it to Pedron. However, I realized that that was impossible.

Pedron had early on regarded it as her own. Once in her hands, she looked at it for nearly a quarter of an hour and then abruptly folded it and put it in her bosom. She bowed deep with gratitude. I noticed that after she had bowed, for no reason at all, she blushed with a sudden flash of shyness.

Princess was even more interesting. She was looking at Pedron from the side and when Pedron bowed she smiled secretively as if she had been spying on a secret affair. She was only sixteen and that smile ought not have been on the face of a sixteen-year-old girl. I caught all of this and was fascinated. The observer sees all. To my surprise, Princess repeated the performance and gave me the same secretive smile, so implicit that I couldn't help blushing.

Time sped by in their company.

In order to show that I was even handed I offered to do a sketch for Princess as well. I was unexpectedly refused.

I thought she was dissatisfied with my picture and that was a blow to my self-esteem. However, I said nothing more because at that moment there was the sound of a third gunshot.

This time, the sound of the gunshot was much closer. Almost simultaneous with the shot there was the sudden resounding bellow of an ox. My whole body shook. I sensed that there had been an accident and without a word to the two women, rushed off in the direction of the gunshot.

All the snow had melted. The damp surface was covered with a mist that was being drawn up by the sun. The graveled waste was not muddy but within a 100 meters my heart was racing unbearably. I slowed to a jogtrot, then to a walk and then halted and collapsed.

In that instant I was gripped by the premonition of an accident which I struggled unsuccessfully to escape. My heart was giving trouble.

My premonition was not wrong.

XV

They came across another herd of wild asses.

Lu Gao warned Little Bai not to shoot wild asses or roebuck.

"The people shoot roebuck. Why can't we? Anyhow, don't supply and marketing firms buy in musk? If you don't shoot deer where does the musk come from?"

"We don't do it." Lu Gao offered no further explanation.

There must have been at least over a hundred wild asses in the herd, a spectacular sight as they galloped about. The fresh snow on the graveled waste had just melted and the herd raised no dust as it galloped by. It was easy to see that Little Bai's hands itched unbearably. If you paid attention to his hands you would discover that his right hand had a firm grip of the downward pointing barrel. His right hand was sweaty. His left subconsciously and continuously gripped and then relaxed in unceasing movement.

The herd seemed to realize that they would not harm them and simply leaped and frolicked nearby. Little Bai felt that they were like spoilt children but the herd took almost no notice of them and could be said to have completely ignored their presence.

"Wouldn't it be wonderful if we could catch a few alive!"

"They're too clever to be caught and very fast. They say even antelopes can't beat them."

"I heard that there were lots of antelopes on the steppe, how is it that in all this time we haven't seen a single one."

Lu Gao laughed: "It's your bad luck."

Scattered here and there in front of them were some small patches of grass. With his sharp eyes, Little Bai spotted a large rodent sticking its head out of a hole amongst the grass. There were others around it.

"Voles! Aiya, so many!"

"They're snow pigs. Also called marmots, quite precious furred animals. There are a lot on the steppe."

"Why doesn't anybody catch them?"

"In Qinghai thousands of people trap them. Then I heard that there had been bubonic plague and that the quarantine and prevention service had forbidden their purchase. They said that several marmot trappers had died. It requires a special skill to trap marmots. They have to be skinned and you have to scrape the fat from the pelt. It's not easy at all."

"But is there really bubonic plague? If there is, why was it that only a few died out of all those thousands? In addition plague is an artificial bacillus and not every natural rodent species carries it. Plague spreads easily and if marmot trappers had really caught it, it would be difficult to control in the country or even in the whole world, it's sheer nonsense."

"The last time I went from Golmud to Xining by train, the carriage was full of marmot trappers, from Gansu and Shaanxi, Sichuan and Ningxia. They were all saying that they were not accepting Marmot pelts in Qinghai Province, you had to go to other provinces. Also, people asked me whether they were accepted in Tibet and were there a lot of marmots there?"

"Ought to talk to foreign trade companies about this and get them to organize the opening up of marmot pelt resources. A few days ago the *People's Daily* reported that national fur exports had declined. It would be a great pity if such a valuable fur resource was not effectively developed!"

Little Bai carried on talking with restrained indignation.

"Teacher Lu, I would really like to do this. You would first set up a fur trading company and then make contact with tanning factories in the interior. After that have garments made up by high class fur companies and arrange exports through foreign trade channels. Really, I want to do it. I've had a letter from a fellow student back at home, he say everybody's resigning and setting up in business."

"Wolf."

"What? I was saying that I've had a letter from a fellow student ..."

"Wolf."

Little Bai saw it now, two wolves, their bellies to the ground, were creeping towards the utterly unaware herd of asses. The one in front had only one ear.

"Teacher Lu, look, only one ear." As he spoke, Little Bai gently raised the rifle. Equally gently, Lu Gao pushed it down. Lu Gao lowered his voice.

"Wait a moment, you'll see a rare sight."

"But the asses haven't discovered them, they'll harm the wild asses."

"Wild asses are the most alert of all animals. They know and are just playing a joke on the wolves."

"Joking with their lives."

"Watch, you don't see this often."

The wolves were less than 10 meters from the nearest ass. One Ear suddenly dashed forward with the other close behind. The ass calmly waited until the moment of the wolf's charge and then fiercely kicked up its rear hooves and flew gracefully away. One Ear had obviously received an injury to its forehead, it retreated and did not attack again; the other wolf reluctantly chased on for a space and stopped when the distance stretched out further and further.

Lu Gao prodded the bemused Little Bai.

"Rifle!"

Little Bai came to with a start, lifted the rifle and pulled the trigger. With pressure. And again with pressure. What's the matter?

Lu Gao reminded him: "Safety catch."

Little Bai put off the safety catch, the two wolves, realizing the presence of people, lowered their bodies and ran off at high speed. Little Bai, unreconciled to lack of success, aimed at the already distant wolves and loosed off two shots after them to send them on their way.

Yao Liang heard these two shots just as he was beginning the portrait of Pedron.

They had come a long way. Lu Gao suggested that they should turn back.

Little Bai's enthusiasm was clearly not yet exhausted. It was no longer early and they ought to return. No sign could be found of the herd of asses that had been nearby. On the way back, Little Bai was dejected.

"Put the safety catch on."

"No. It'll save time in case of any more wild animals."

"That won't do. Put it on. Somebody could get hurt if it goes off accidentally."

Unwillingly, Little Bai put the safety catch on, inwardly cursing Lu Gao as a coward. Frightened to death. Frightened that if it goes off it'll injure you, isn't that it. He no longer had any interest in talking about the fantasy of resigning and going into business.

During this dreary section of the journey, a passing cloud delivered itself of a hail storm, the hailstones were larger than those normally seen in the interior, about the size of a peanut, very painful when they struck the head. Lu Gao and Little Bai had no option but to take off their jackets, wrap them round their heads and stand still. Little Bai took the opportunity to vent his spleen in a different direction and cursed heaven as a shameless bastard.

Lu Gao paid him no attention. Let him curse one for the other and get it off his chest.

On the way back they met some deer. Little Bai simply made a face and wouldn't look at them, energetically kicking at every little stone in his path. Can't shoot. Won't shoot.

Lu Gao conscientiously picked up two trunks of crawling pine and carried them on his back. Little Bai did not lift a finger to help him.

"People! Teacher Lu."

"Where?"

Lu Gao saw the two yaks in the distance.

"They're probably Choegyal's yaks," Little Bai said.

"No. Too large. They look like wild yaks."

"Wild yaks?"

Little Bai's spirits rose, he took up the rifle and rapidly made off in the direction of the yaks. Lu Gao stood aghast.

"Little Bai, don't be a fool, give me the gun!"

"Why? Am I that useless?"

Little Bai turned his head to ask Lu Gao, his expression and tone of voice filled with suppressed fury. Lu Gao was gob-smacked and didn't know what to say for the best.

"What's up with you, Little Bai, that wasn't what I meant."

"What do you mean? That I'm useless and it's only you that's any use, huh?"

Little Bai said no more, turned away and carried on walking rapidly. Lu Gao stood motionless for a long while. He could not be angry with Little Bai. He was the leader of the group and elder brother. Little Bai had always called him Teacher Lu.

After a while he suddenly came to his senses and loosed his hold on the firewood he was carrying, dropping it to the ground. Little Bai was now some distance away and he would have to run to catch him up.

His heart was palpitating and he was gasping for breath. He couldn't run very fast.

He thought of shouting to Little Bai to stop but Little Bai's abuse made his sense of self-respect prevent him from shouting.

Little Bai was 200 meters ahead. A further 200 meters ahead of him were the two yaks. The one furthest from him was a bull. Huge in body and calm in appearance. It was his enormous size that gave him self-confidence and a sense of security. On this plateau there was no other animal that was a direct threat to him. The brown bear and leopard fled at the sight of him. He weighed around 1,500 kilos, say a ton. An enraged wild yak on the attack was very fast and could toss a fleeing slim-legged wolf on to its huge curved horns in a trice.

Lu Gao's nerves were stretched to their limit. Almost tearing apart his vocal chords he shouted to Little Bai the moment he raised his rifle: "Don't shoot! Absolutely don't shoot!"

Little Bai calmly turned and looked at him with utter contempt. He then knelt on one knee, took aim and methodically pulled the trigger.

Lu Gao knew it was too late, the end lay in the hands of heaven.

Stunned, he waited for the yak to react. His senses were half-numbed and abnormally dull.

A gunshot. Then an ear-splitting bellow.

Perhaps it was the confused sound that brought him back to normality.

He saw the bull yak's body judder a moment while the cow turned and escaped, emitting a low bellow as it ran. Thereafter, everything that he had foreseen took place.

The bull regained its balance, faced Little Bai head-on, kicked up its heels fiercely and launched itself like an arrow. Lu Gao knew instinctively that it was over, completely over.

If the shot had struck a vulnerable point it would have been Little Bai's good fortune. Otherwise it was a lucky escape. To escape the horns of an enraged bull yak perhaps meant that there was no other disaster that could harm him. Lu Gao held not the slightest hope of this but in his sub-conscious there was still a certain factor that controlled his actions and he deftly took off his old wind-cheater. In truth he was awaiting the appearance of a miracle. So once more he roared.

"Ahhhh—" A sound that exhausted his lungs.

No matter what the outcome of the first attack on Little Bai, Lu Gao's idea of attracting the attention of the yak was born of commitment. The maddened yak did not attack Little Bai for the second time and turned its anger towards Lu Gao.

Lu Gao had not the time to consider Little Bai. He didn't know what state Little Bai was in after the first attack. All he knew was that he was in a passive position and that the yak had charged Little Bai once. It was difficult to imagine that any life remained beneath the hooves of that monster. Lu Gao could not think of this or of anything. He had to put his whole mind to dealing with the wild yak.

The yak snorted roughly and pawed the ground but did not attack straight away. Lu Gao's mind was extraordinarily clear, he even seemed to feel not the least fear. He grasped the collar and the hem of the wind-cheater in either hand. He calmly gazed at the wild yak, his mind completely empty. Lu Gao knew for certain that the first time he fell into this situation he would have no choice—no choice at all—he could only wait. A life experience that could not be repeated.

It is hard to say how long this lasted, perhaps it was a matter of seconds, or it may have been much longer. Lu Gao lost any conception of time, it was of no use or significance to him. It was the first time that he had faced an absolute, pure void that did not include time.

It charged once more, more fiercely, more confidently and with more intention than before. It intended to force him into a fatal position. He waited its arrival without moving. At the last moment he raised both arms, flourished the wind-cheater and in a flash swiftly stepped aside and fell to the ground.

The yak's horns caught the wind-cheater and it charged on. The wind-cheater obstructed its vision. Bellowing, it threw its head from side to side until it had tossed the wind-cheater on to its neck. The cow now started a distant plaintive bellowing. The yak, no longer enraged, no longer interested in its two fallen enemies, galloped swiftly away on its enormous hooves.

XVI

It was fortunate that you kept a diary during those days of desperate confusion. Only on the basis of the diary were you eventually just able to extract a thread of an outline of the time. If you had to put down the diary and were asked which day you went to Lake Manasarovar, would you be able to answer clearly?

You would be able to say that that this was the day Dadra remembered very clearly without a diary entry, Dadra had been looking forward to this day for a very long time.

You only stayed in Burang for a week. As you drove through the night to Burang you swore that you would sleep night and day for ten days when you arrived. You were tired out but you only stayed there a week. Dadra wouldn't stay on and Migmar was clamoring to go.

It was quite simple. Lake Manasarovar and Mount Kailash were only a day's journey by truck from Burang. After so much hardship it was this that Dadra wanted.

It was dark by the time that you reached Lake Manasarovar, you couldn't make out the lunar calendar but you remember that it was an upper crescent moon. You thought that an upper crescent moon should be a new moon; an old moon was bound to be a lower crescent moon.

To save money you all simply slept in the truck. At night the sound of the lake was by no means peaceful and waves broke on the shore with some little noise. You asked Lu Gao whether you would be going to Mount Kailash the next day. He replied that you would discuss it when you got up next morning.

It was cold at night by the lakeside, deep in your sleeping bags you hardly dared stick your head out. It was lonely in the cold of night and nobody felt like talking. Because you were not sufficiently rested at Burang and had not made up for the exhaustion of the last ten days, once you were in your sleeping bag you slept like the dead. If anything had happened during the night you wouldn't have known.

You woke at dawn and were the first to be awake. Lu Gao was asleep and so were Dadra and Migmar. You didn't want to get up and were even reluctant to move, you just closed your eyes again and dozed. The air was freezing and your face was so cold that it wrinkled. You snuggled deep into the sleeping bag, head and all.

It was Migmar talking to Dadra in Tibetan.

You couldn't hear properly or understand. It had probably little to do with you. You could hear Migmar's concern in his tone of voice and for a long while Dadra said nothing. At last he said something and to your dismay you discovered that his voice was lifeless and trembling.

When you got up, Lu Gao told you in confidence that Dadra and Migmar had been into the water during the night. They had insisted on bathing in the middle of the night as if this was an act of reverence. When they got back Dadra had started shivering and had been unable to go to sleep. Lu Gao said that he probably had a fever. However, he also said that you weren't to mention fever to him at all, it would make him angry and lead to conflict. In the eyes of Buddhists, bathing in the holy lake was sacred and not for discussion.

Consequently you said nothing, but you were careful to greet him. Dadra struggled up but you pushed him down.

"There's no hurry to get up, wait until food is ready."

"I've been really tired these last few days."

"Yes, we're all tired out. The scenery here is beautiful, we'll just stay a few days and we can do some painting."

Migmar interjected: "I said there was no hurry to go but he's afraid that you are in a hurry to get to Zanda. He says that we could go round Mount Kailash today and leave this afternoon or early tomorrow morning."

"There's no hurry. We've all been rushing around these last few days and there's been no time at all for painting. So far there's not been a single painting in color from the four of us, what would we have to say for ourselves when we got back? Each of us should do two paintings here before we leave."

"Teacher Lu's back, why not talk to him."

"Old Lu," when you were talking to Lu Gao you had your back to Migmar and Dadra. You gave him a look as you talked to him.

"We're all tired. Why don't we stay here for a couple of days, Dadra can go round the sacred mountain and we can do a couple of paintings. I've just talked to Migmar about it and he thinks the same. That's right Migmar, isn't it?"

"Mm." Migmar looked at Dadra.

Lu Gao said: "That's what I thought, I was thinking of talking to everybody about it. We should all have a good rest."

Huo'er is not far off. Go and stay there.

The beach of the lake was a mixture of grass and shingle. With your portfolios on your backs the three of you came to a slight rise. On its green slopes there was a flock of snow-white sheep.

You looked uneasily across the lake at the long spread of the distant Himalayas. In comparison, the Himalayas towered majestically above the Gangdise range behind you. Himalayas was an abstract term in the minds of many. As a child you had sketched its outline in your drawing book from your imagination. Now they stretched unbroken before you for a thousand miles. You knew now that there was no sketchbook or paper or canvas that could contain them.

You turned to Migmar and remarked: "Migmar, does that snow covered mountain opposite have a name?"

"Aren't they the Himalayas? Why do you ask?"

"I mean the highest one."

The pinnacle of its white summit stood gracefully head and shoulders above the other peaks. Migmar didn't know its name.

You said: "It's much higher than Mount Kailash."

"The surrounding peaks are also higher than Kailash. Kailash is just over 22,000 feet but that one is the king of mountains."

A sacred mountain. It's not the height that matters. It's where there are immortals that matters.

Lu Gao was a little distance away and had heard your conversation.

"It's Mount Langmunani."

"Who told you?"

"Li Jiajun writes about it in his *Travels in Tibet*, there's a passage about the legend of its love for Kailash."

"But she's a whole lot higher than Kailash."

"Nowadays girls all wear high heels," Migmar said with a laugh. "Girls are getting taller and taller."

Lu Gao suddenly changed the subject.

"Migmar, you two went in the lake last night."

Migmar was at a loss.

"Dadra wanted to go in."

"It's too cold at night. You'd better take something to stave off a cold."

"I'm fine."

"You'd better go back. There's medicine in my bag. Find the paracetamol. Take one and give two to Dadra."

Migmar folded his portfolio and went back. You didn't want to ask why he had raised midnight bathing again. When Migmar was some way off in the distance, Lu Gao suddenly shouted at him to stop and caught him up.

"Don't mention that I know you went into the lake. Just give him a couple of pills, don't say any more."

"I know, I won't say anything."

Dadra lay asleep in bed all day and didn't go round the sacred mountain.

You stayed in Huo'er for two days. Apart from cooking and eating you and Lu Gao spent the remaining daylight hours painting. In all you painted three studies in oils. You still felt that there was a lack of ideal composition but that you had to do something while you were there.

On the morning of the third day you received a telegram from the Artists' Association.

Text: Hurry and proceed to Guge without delay.

Lu Gao discussed this with you. Whether it was possible to hurry on now that Dadra was in better spirits. You had delayed too long when the vehicle was stuck and you needed to get on.

You said: "He still has a cough and his nose is running."

"See what he thinks."

You went back and showed the telegram to Migmar and Dadra.

"Then we must go to Zanda today."

Migmar sounded out Dadra: "Can you manage?"

Dadra looked at Migmar furiously: "Why should I not manage?!"

You laughed inwardly. Dadra clearly believed that he had completely concealed his illness from you and Lu Gao. Good.

You asked tentatively, what about the circuit of the sacred mountain? Lu Gao turned and looked at Dadra enquiringly, waiting for his views.

Dadra thought for a moment.

"Let's do it this way. There are a lot of people here who come to pay their respects to Buddha, I could find them and give them money to go round for me. Otherwise going round will delay us another two days. It will be enough if I'm there in my mind."

Migmar and Dadra each bought an expensive plastic container for 12 yuan. They filled them to the top with water from the sacred lake to take back to friends and relatives. They stopped for an hour on the road past Mount Kailash and they both spent ten yuan on a Buddhist devotee who would make a circuit of the holy mountain for them.

You asked Migmar dubiously: "Would they take the money but not do the circuit? We'll have gone and won't know."

Migmar said: "Dadra said they wouldn't. They were all believers and would not deceive Buddha. If they did deceive him they would be punished." Migmar was not too devout but adopted an attitude of pretended seriousness when speaking.

XVII

As he made his way over Lu Gao's heart shrank. He had not seen Little Bai move after the wild yak's attack. At that moment, I was lying on my side on the gravel about 1,000 meters away. Had Lu Gao known at the time that I was also in mortal danger he would have broken down.

It was my good luck that I had not run too far. Pedron and Princess were by the tent and they could still see me. They started running towards me almost the moment I dropped.

My heart was beating madly, it was unbearable. The two women were frightened out of their wits. My mind was clear, it was a coronary attack. I gestured that they should fetch the medical bag. Princess understood and rushed back.

Pedron helped me to sit up and I was almost completely supported in her embrace. Her breath warmed my scalp with an extremely pleasant tickling sensation. Water vapor was still rising from the ground.

I could feel her rounded body through the single layer of clothing. I could not move nor wanted to move but just looked at her two large, plump but wrinkled hands. The two hands held me as one's own child is held, neither tightly nor loosely. I wanted to turn and smell her warm breath and find the lips from which it came, at that moment Princess came running up. I didn't turn to see but heard the sound of her hurried footsteps.

I found the nitroglycerine for coronary disease in the bag and swallowed it in my own saliva. Pedron still held me and I sat quietly in her embrace.

Princess crouched opposite and also seemed really anxious for me. She was flushed from running and beads of sweat covered her rosy face. She didn't bother to wipe them away.

I quietly said: "Thank you Princess."

I heard the sound of my voice in the distance as if it were floating in a dream. I probably only understood what was said because it was myself who was speaking. Princess did not respond, either because I actually hadn't spoken or because she couldn't understand a word of my Chinese.

I sat like this for a long time and when I felt a little better tried to struggle to my feet. Of course, it was no good. Pedron still held me and with Princess's help, got me to my feet with some difficulty. It took about half an hour for us to travel a distance of around 100 meters. They supported me on either side and with my arms round their necks, they took the weight of almost my whole body. They walked and my feet dragged behind them.

Eventually, we arrived. I collapsed on to the bed, my breathing intermittent.

Perhaps because of lack of oxygen or because of illness my senses had been dulled. It was only now that I thought of Lu Gao and Little Bai. I gestured to them to go and look. Pedron said something to Princess who gestured to me that she would go and look. I nodded with relief and felt a sudden wave of exhaustion. I closed my eyes and probably fell asleep at once. I am embarrassed to describe what I felt as I slept, what happened later may have had its roots in that sleep but I can't explain it. I have no way of knowing what she thought about it but I know myself. The guilt will be with me for the rest of my life.

I can also say that I knew nothing when I was asleep.

The first thing that I heard when I woke up was the sound of groaning. I forced my eyes open. Lu Gao was kneeling by the bed with his back to me. The groaning came from Little Bai. With an effort I recalled what had just happened; I remembered the gunshot, the bellowing yak; I remembered being embraced by Pedron. Had I fallen asleep? How was Little Bai?

"Lu, what's the matter, has Little Bai had an accident?"

Lu Gao looked round, an appalled look on his face. However he managed a smile. I was able to sense that that smile derived from heartfelt joy. I smiled too. Two old friends, the Ali wilderness, in the middle of the night with the waning moon shining into the tent.

> Lu Gao and I were on the salt flats, he had his double-barreled shotgun over his shoulder. The air was filled with a vague booming noise.
>
> "Brother Lu, can you hear the sound of waves?"
>
> Didn't he hear what I had said? We were several miles from the sea, why were my eardrums

always filled with the booming sound of waves? A long-tailed rabbit darted out of the grass in front of me, the white tuft on its tail wagging.

"Brother Lu, that proverb about a rabbit's tail never growing should be changed. On the steppe even rabbits' tails grow."

Long-tailed rabbits were much smaller than ordinary rabbits, it was their tails that were unusual, they were about seven or eight inches long. Lu Gao did not shoot this kind of small animal. Sometimes, amongst the sparse and neglected outskirts of a village, you came across a solitary tomb. That red-coated fox disappeared behind the tomb in the twinkling of an eye. We hurried to the spot and I found a hole by the tomb the width of the mouth of a bowl. I gathered up some dry grass and lit it in the hole and smoked out the fox which was shot to pieces by Lu Gao. I went to pick it up but he wouldn't let me. He tossed the dead fox into the ebbing tide in a ditch so that it could be carried out to the Bohai Sea and then into the Pacific. I said many times that this was a pity.

I couldn't get up I felt so weak that it was difficult to move. Little Bai groaned ceaselessly, Lu Gao said that the yak had gored Little Bai in two places, in the ribs where there was only a shallow wound; and in the thigh, a six-inch-long incision deep enough to reveal the bone.

"Princess helped me to get him back. He has a charmed life, even a maddened yak couldn't finish him off. We also owe thanks to Princess, she burst into tears when she saw Little Bai as wounded as he was. She insisted on carrying him here on her back, I couldn't dissuade her. Little Bai was in shock and knew nothing."

A sad smile appeared on Lu Gao's face. An expression that made me feel a stranger. I thought there must be something wrong with my feelings. I was terribly weak and kept hallucinating. Lu Gao hadn't slept at all.

"Little Bai has a charmed life. It's a surprise he wasn't trampled to death by the yak, I expected him to be trampled to a pulp. That yak was huge."

> We were working in the paddy fields, the water was level. Lu Gao's pet dog, Lu Erh was lying on the bank. Lu Gao and I were shoveling mud from the same square paddy field with a bucket. A passing educated youth called Lu Erh several times but Lu Erh made not the slightest response and the youth passed resentfully on. Lu Gao then called: "Lu Erh." The dog raised his head alertly, waiting for a command. "Fetch the water bottle." Lu Erh bounded away and returned several minutes later with Lu Gao's old army water bottle held in its mouth. Lu Gao twisted the stopper from the bottle with his teeth, took a large mouthful and then passed the flask to me.
>
> Then it was Lu Gao and I at night. We cut off Ingus's head with a sharp knife. Ingus was a vicious dog that belonged to the army cook of a neighboring brigade farm, a huge fierce wolf of an animal. We waited five nights and had just strangled him. Lu Gao called to Le Erh and squatted down and took Le Erh's head in his hands and held his face close to Lu Erh's. He didn't shed a single tear. He told me to go and dig a deep hole on the salt flats. He strangled Lu Erh and cut off his head. Afterwards he told me to bury Ingus's head with Lu Erh's body. We spent the night skinning Ingus and boiled

his flesh in a large pot and called up all the educated youth for a feast. Strangely enough it rained heavily that night and the place where the salt flat had been dug up was flattened by the rain so that there was no trace. Even I couldn't accurately find the place where the dog had been buried. I left the village earlier than Lu Gao. Two years later I went to see him. We were drinking and chatting and eventually got drunk, when he asked: "I never asked you, but where is Lu Erh buried?" I forget how I replied. Lu Erh's yellowed skull hangs on one of the beams of his hut. I am a little superstitious.

Early next morning Pedron and Princess came over with some medicine. It was musk and a bone snuff bottle. They made the musk into a powder which they put into the wound on Little Bai's thigh, Little Bai cried out in pain and unaware, tightly grasped Princess's hand. They re-bandaged his wound and he quietened down and was soon fast asleep. Pedron ground the snuff bottle against a stone and moistened it with the little fresh water that remained. The resulting water was very dirty but Pedron firmly forced apart Little Bai's teeth and poured the water in.

I lay there hopelessly. Lu Gao sat alongside taking no part or doing anything, leaving the two women to attend to Little Bai.

Later they realized that we hadn't eaten. Pedron found the bag of rice and poured its contents into the pressure cooker and took it to the river to rinse the rice. Princess found a tin and the tin opener and put them in Lu Gao's hands to open. Lu Gao absent mindedly took them and mechanically rotated the opener. Princess washed yesterday's mushrooms and tore them into strips in exactly the same way. She lit the fire and cooked them in a pan.

Pedron's rice was half-cooked but Princess's soup was delicious. Whatever you say, it was not at all not easy to come by this meal and it was thanks to them. Pedron fed Little Bai. I rather wanted Princess to feed him. Lu Gao ate nothing and sat there blankly.

I said: "Old Lu, have a nap, you haven't slept all night."

He was obviously thinking of something. He made no response.

> We took Lu Erh to the Ling River ferry. I asked how far we were away from the sea. Lu Gao said less than 13 *li*. He said that at high tide the sea water would come flooding in. The river was wide and calm at this point. We boarded the ferry. It was the beginning of August and although it was the evening the weather was still sultry. I took of my clothes and dived in, wonderful! Bewitched, Lu Erh jumped in too and paddled happily about. Lu Gao steered the boat and followed close behind me. I enjoyed myself and simply swam back and told Lu Gao to wait for me on the opposite bank. The water surface began to get choppy and twilight had set in over the waste. I floated, face up, on the water and thought of a carefree marble rolling on the top of the dyke. I didn't realize that the wind had risen. I was floating on the surface. Floating on the water is the best form of exercise, especially in a river where both banks are clothed in green, you can imagine nothing better. After taking a couple of mouthfuls of water I turned over and began to do the breast stroke and discovered that sea water had come in with the tide, the water tasted brackish. Lu Erh was barking in the distance on the opposite bank. Lu Gao was calling me. It was dark on the surface of the water and he couldn't see me. I replied and immediately choked on a mouthful of water. I was really nervous, the first

time I had feared for my life. I paddled with all my strength but the swell in the water prevented me from reaching the bank. I hadn't enough confidence and my arms ached, I swallowed more water and Lu Gao appeared in the water not far from me, swimming towards me. I felt that I was finished and prayed that he would come closer so that I could grab hold of him but he didn't and just swam alongside and told me to calm down and keep swimming and not to give up. I couldn't grab hold of him and could only paddle and got to the bank by myself like this. He was right, if he had let me hold on to him we both would have been finished. I would have been finished and would have dragged him down with me. Once on the bank I was scared stiff. The moon had just appeared over the horizon, large and round. The waves on the river surged to over a meter in height, it was a lunar spring tide. And high wind as well. The wind from the south helped the tide. Extremely dangerous. That's all he said. Lu Erh didn't bark again. That was well over ten years ago. We were so young then.

Lu Gao squirrelled into his sleeping bag and lay down.

Princess half knelt and half sat in front of Little Bai with a look of maternal concern and tenderness on her face. Little Bai was clearly deeply asleep, I could only see the back of his head.

The sun shone brightly and the ground outside started to radiate heat. I dragged myself upright in my sleeping bag and when Pedron who had been washing the bowls saw me, she rushed over and helped me up and out into the sun outside. It was cold and miserable in the tent. The sun made me feel affectionate. I walked slowly with Pedron's support. We saw another herd of wild asses.

Filled with curiosity the wild asses came closer, pawing at

the ground and neighing playfully. My mind was utterly relaxed. We turned to the northern side of the tent. With the right hand that lay across Pedron's shoulders I tightly embraced her neck and turned her head towards me clamping my dry lips on hers and fiercely sucking like somebody parched with thirst who suddenly discovers water. Our bodies were pressed together.

To start with she was passive as I kissed her, but later, as if aroused, she responded with passionate kisses that had an impulse that seemed to want to swallow me whole. I felt her body heavily pressed convulsively on mine, the desire to become one completely overwhelming me. I now realized that what had happened in my feverish sleep the previous night had been no illusion. It had been her hands. Later it had been her body. Yes. True. Absolutely no mistake. Now that I was awake I knew without doubt that this hand was last night's hand; and that this body was last night's body. The sun shone bright, warm and with warmth. The sun was brimming with desire. And the herd of wild asses surrounded us.

Lu Gao would not get up. He wouldn't get up immediately having just gone to sleep. Princess was taking the opportunity of the absence of others to get closer to Little Bai. Perhaps secretly kissing his closed eyes, perhaps doing a little something else. I didn't care, we didn't care. The feelings that I had encountered when asleep became reality. We re-enacted all that had seemed illusory the previous night. My daughter. Now was not the time to think of my daughter. Pedron was so beautiful. So beautiful. So beautiful. Oh.

What is it with me? Oh. Oh. Oh.

XVIII

Yao Liang recovered very quickly and by the afternoon could walk by himself. He realized, first, that they were short of water. Who could go and fetch it? Lu Gao was still asleep. He decided that he could walk there slowly and taking up the plastic can quietly slipped out of the tent. He slowly made his way up a small hill in the direction from which they fetched water. The hill gradually flattened out. Walking down the slope saved energy and Yao Liang felt that fetching water was no great hardship.

This was the fourth day. Yao Liang thought of the interesting fact that in those four days the three artists had done one drawing and one sketch between them. Then he saw them. Perhaps he should do a color drawing of them but he couldn't see what artistic interest they had. It was those two, absolutely no mistake. That One Ear. The hairs on the back of Yao Liang's neck rose. They appeared to have no great interest in him. They kept slightly back on a parallel course about 100 meters to his right, at arm's length so to speak. Pay them no attention.

Yao Liang thought of the letter that he had received from his wife just before they had set out. She had said that their daughter had registered to attend school. It was now the 22nd of August, and school started on 1st September. Another nine days, where would he be in nine days' time? Still here perhaps. Hard to say. Perhaps they would already have arrived at Guge. One should not be too optimistic, of course, nor too pessimistic either. You could see the sea. Tibetans called lake sea—co. Lake Yamzho Yumco (Lake Yamdrok). Lake Mapam Yumco. This sea was not very big. They were still on their parallel course 100 meters behind though. Yao Liang no longer felt so weak. He thought that if they dared to come forward he could beat them off with the water can. His daughter had also written him a letter. His wife said that she already knew how to write more than 100 characters. His daughter's letter was very short: "Baba, (a much exaggerated comma) I miss you." No. No! Don't think of Pedron. He must do one in color when he got back. A picture of this cold, indifferent, barren, neglected waste. But would they really be rescued? Did he really believe that Dadra and the others would get out? He was not totally sure of himself. They were still 100 meters off on his right and slightly behind. Stop and wait a moment for them.

They stopped too. Why didn't they call or howl? Did they still not know of the awesome effect of a wolf's howl? Perhaps.

The sea was a brilliant blue and calmer than normal, not the slightest ripple. Yao Yuan felt that he had produced a fantasy of his own. He saw the snow covered mountains across the sea. The Himalayas. But he saw, imprinted upon the snow of these mountains, an enormous market, as busy and bustling as the Barkhor, the people who thronged it, however, were wearing turbans, like the Muslims of Western Asia or North Africa. Illusion. He would rather close his eyes, the feeling that he was hallucinating would erode his self-confidence and self-control. He would rather avoid any illusion. He was bewitched once more and thought only of getting in the water. Of crossing the sea. The sea was too blue, too seductive. He kept going and when he turned his head, saw that they too were walking towards the sea. Market. Illusion. He could think of nothing else. If he thought for a moment, there would be a different conclusion. Why could it not be a mirage? He couldn't think and so was unable to think this far. He was just determined to walk into the water he was influenced by some formless enchantment. He stepped into the blue water. The surface of the lake was a pure sky blue. His feet splashed into the water and the spell was broken. The sensation of cold fresh water returned him to normality.

They were standing still too. Looking at him, seemingly without much interest. Fill up with water. He bent and half-filled the can, rinsed and poured it out. They lowered their heads and drank normally. Without tarrying he filled up the can and returned to the shore. They had finished drinking and set out on the return journey almost at the same time as he did.

The wonder lay not in the fact that with the utmost care he had spilled as little water as possible, nor in the fatigue that he felt as he slowly trudged uphill. Like the others he felt that fetching water was not an easy job. However, he had the strength, he had walked nearly 20 *li, c*arrying a can of water on the way back and had not felt that it was too unmanageable. In the end, he had brought the water back. No, the wonder did not lie here.

It was dark but Lu Gao was still asleep. So was Little Bai. He should cook for them. No. There was no rice, so strictly speaking he should get them something to eat. There was a little half-cooked rice stuck to the bottom of the pan. Yao Liang lit the fire, broke up the scorched rice, added water and heated it under pressure in the pressure cooker. What else to add? That's it. Fish. Semi-dried fish. Yao Liang fried the fish to a yellow delicacy. He then called to Lu Gao and woke up Little Bai. Lu Gao sat up, rubbing his eyes.

"Old Yao, what's that noise?"

Only then did Yao Liang notice the sound of howling that filled the air. At once he thought of the two wolves. It was bound to be them.

"One Ear and the other followed me when I went to fetch water, they followed me back without a sound."

Lu Gao finished up the scorched rice and fish without saying a word. Yao Liang thought of reminding him that Little Bai hadn't had anything to eat yet but the words never left his mouth. He eat a couple of fish, they weren't salty.

Little Bai was gazing at the roof of the tent, silently and not groaning.

"Little Bai, have something to eat, there's fried fish."

Yao Liang put the fish in front of Little Bai. Rather unwillingly Little Bai poked an arm out of the sleeping bag, grabbed a fish and began to eat it.

Yao Liang turned to Lu Gao.

"Old Lu, what are we going to do? There's no food."

At that that moment Little Bai was suddenly sick behind them.

"What's the matter? What's the matter, Little Bai?"

With some difficulty Little Bai stopped vomiting and passed the fish he had in his hand to Yao Liang, shaking his head and withdrawing his arm back into the sleeping bag. Yao Liang realized that his injury was too serious and that he couldn't stand the smell of fish. But what was to be done? There was no rice, what could he eat?

Yao Liang turned over their stores and found and opened their only tin of tangerines and put it to Little Bai's lips. Without opening his eyes Little Bai shook his head in refusal. He asked: "Is that a wolf howling?"

"Yes, it's One Ear."

Little Bai clearly had no interest in the answer and looked as if he had fallen asleep. Yao Liang put the cold fried fish in the embers to cook where it sizzled away. He ate two medium sized ones, and felt that the fishy smell might make him sick too. What were they going to do tonight? Who would stand guard? Little Bai was obviously not fit.

"Old Lu, Old Lu. Have you gone to sleep again?"

Lu Gao's eyes were blurred, what was the matter with him? He had changed.

"Old Lu, pull yourself together. What are we going to do tonight? Who's going to stand guard? Also, we're out of rice and firewood too, tomorrow ..." Yao Liang watched Lu Gao push himself to his feet, put on his overcoat and sling the gun over his shoulder. Yao Liang said no more.

"You go to sleep, keep an eye on Little Bai. I'll stand guard."

Lu Gao finished and went out into the darkness.

The howling became stronger and stronger, its sound particularly ear-piercing. Yao Liang decided to take no notice of them. He lit the pressure lamp, found the exercise-book and wrote up his diary. Little Bai was saying something. Yao Liang turned his head to look. He was talking in his sleep. Under the strong light of the pressure lamp his face looked even whiter. Yao Liang knew that because he had lost so much blood he needed something nourishing, such as chicken, make him some chicken soup. That's it, weren't there chickens round here? Think about it, the first thing to do early tomorrow morning was to go bird shooting.

Yao Liang continued to write his diary.

One Ear and his wife continued to howl.

Little Bai continued to sleep.

What was Lu Gao doing? He hadn't returned to the tent.

Lu Gao had gone to see Choegyal.

When Lu Gao knocked on the door Choegyal was drinking tea.

Princess opened the door and smiled happily at Lu Gao. Lu Gao stood by the door and Choegyal looked up and saw who it was. The two men looked at each other expressionlessly for nearly three seconds.

"*Qing jin*—please come in."

Lu Gao was apparently unsurprised by Choegyal's Chinese.

Pedron was doing something in the corner and looked up furtively at Lu Gao. Lu Gao thought before he spoke.

"… I wonder, if we could borrow a little *tsamba*. We've no food."

"We don't have much. Pedron is packing up some rice for you."

"Rice? Where from?"

"In exchange for goats. Pedron's going to have a child. It's for when she gives birth. Four goats in exchange for 20 catties."

"We can't take it. I was just thinking of borrowing a little *tsamba*."

"You won't be able to eat *tsamba*. In any case, we don't have much. I go to Burang once a year and barter a year's food."

Lu Gao turned: "Sorry to have disturbed you."

Lu Gao walked back in deep silence. The night was heavy with darkness, perhaps it was going to snow again. Strangely, there was not a breath of wind and so although the wolves were far away, their howling sounded clear and mournful. Lu Gao didn't return to the tent but sat by the river hoping that it would start snowing.

In the morning the sky was clear. Lu Gao told Yao Liang that Choegyal could speak Chinese. Yao Liang thought of that night. No wonder Choegyal had given Yao Liang such a strange look after he had heard him talking. Lu Gao said nothing about borrowing *tsamba*.

"Old Lu, Little Bai is only semi-conscious, he's in a void. Couldn't you go and shoot something, preferably a bird, to make a nourishing soup for him? Otherwise it'll be awful for him."

"I've seen nothing but black-necked cranes these last few days."

"But Little Bai is in a very bad way."

Lu Gao said nothing more.

"Old Lu if you won't shoot I will. If it's illegal punish me. Is this the time to be talking of f--king animal protection?"

Lu Gao still said nothing, Yao Liang felt the heat of fury on his forehead, how had Lu Gao became so useless so quickly? Because he was the leader of the group? Or because Little Bai had argued with him? Yao Liang picked up the gun, quietly went over to where Little Bai lay asleep unconscious, tucked in his sleeping bag and covered him with an overcoat. Just as he turned to leave, Lu Gao spoke up in an indifferent tone.

"I know all about you and Pedron."

"What if you do? I don't care!"

"You may not know it but Pedron's pregnant."

Yao Liang stood stock still and for a long time said not a word.

"You, who told you?"

"I went to borrow some *tsamba*, Choegyal told me."

"Borrow *tsamba*? Why didn't you say so? He wouldn't lend any?"

"He wanted me to take the rice put aside for Pedron's pregnancy."

"We couldn't accept that!"

"I didn't, so I came back empty handed."

Yao Liang did not know what to say. He stood for a moment and then walked heavily out into the wilderness.

His luck was good. He hadn't gone far when the first flock of black-necked cranes came flying low towards him. They flew with a graceful disdain, utterly unprepared for the armed Yao

Liang beneath them. Yao Liang was in a bad mood, and in no frame of mind to take any pleasure or even to think more. He raised the gun and, almost without aiming, pulled the trigger. A large crane fell in response to the shot. Yao Liang's mind was numb but he felt that there was something incomprehensible; the crane had died too lightly, its wings had hardly flapped.

When he shot the crane, he had not thought of Pedron.

XIX

Fascinating. It was night-time when you reached Burang. You almost always reached your over-night stops at night. In haste during daylight and anxious to travel another ten or more kilometers when darkness fell. The odometer says that from the place where the truck was stuck to Burang is 224 kilometers. From the time you set out at ten in the morning you were on the road for a good 17 hours. When you reached Burang you first tried to find the hospital. You probably did not suffer the most, Little Bai's injury was much more serious. But you were in a bad way too. Your wound had opened up and blood had soaked the bandages to form a very thick scab. You had screamed throughout the journey so that the driver dared not allow the vehicle the least jolt.

The Burang hospital is not large, it only has two wards. You and Little Bai were installed in the same ward. The resident doctor was very young and had just graduated from Sichuan Medical College. He was called Ji Mei. You all got on very well with him the few days you were there. He was shocked when he asked you about your condition. He said it was beyond belief. However, he said it was a miracle, there was no problem, once the stitches had been removed you would be fine. Later events demonstrated that there was a sufficient scientific basis to what he said. But you only have to recall the jolting of that road to give an involuntary shudder. That feeling will simply prevent you ever forgetting.

According to Migmar, Lu Gao sleeps almost all day. You are curious as to why, although you were totally exhausted, you slept so little during those seven days. During the day, Ji Mei and Migmar come to see you (Dadra comes occasionally, sits for a while and then goes), and time passes easily. It's just at night when you can't sleep that your imagination runs wild.

You think of your daughter. Her little hands are long and slender like her mother's. She can write characters, and write a letter too.

You think of your mother. You ought to write to her. Normally, letter writing is what you least like doing. In the end however, your mother is always your mother. Last year and the year before, for many years in fact—you were not well off and you never gave your mother any filial financial support. Your parents' income was not inconsiderable and they did not need your money. But what were you thinking of? You were their son. You thereupon decided to send your mother 100 yuan before the New Year. Working here you receive a local allowance, several tens of yuan more than you receive at home in the interior. Your wife won't object, she's very understanding, it's just that back in the interior you were hard-pressed for money and though the heart was willing the flesh was weak. That's decided then, but you are still not sleepy.

Think of something else.

Pedron. Lu Gao said that Pedron was pregnant and that it was Choegyal who had told him. You are astonished. It simply wasn't visible. But what's to be done? To start with you thought that Pedron was over 30, in fact, she was very young indeed. Her enthusiasm was absolutely that of a young girl, you will never forget Pedron with her eyes misty with passion. You cannot imagine the circumstances under which you might meet again. That is, if you were able to visit Ali again and if you were able to see her.

You will probably always be ensnared by those two wolves. Even in another place and time you can still hear their strange howling. It's them, no mistake. You know too well the characteristically suggestive sound of One Ear. But could they really be in Burang? It's beyond comprehension.

If the wind now rattles the shutters, you remember what Ji Mei told you about robbers. Your impression of Burang is of a place where the wind blows all day. Its sound makes you uneasy and then twitchy. You cannot even distinguish the difference between the sound of the wind and the howling of the wolves. In recent years, bandits and robbers, said to be border inhabitants of mixed race, have come and gone here. Ji Mei says that in some mud-brick huts it is often possible to buy a revolver for about 60 yuan. No, don't think, you ought to sleep. 60 yuan is not expensive, a single-barreled shot-gun would be more than 100 yuan, if … No you can't buy one if you do you can't use it private ownership of guns is not permitted but Pedron is really pregnant. It's true Lu Gao said so Lu Gao has never told a lie but what's up with Lu Gao is he going to carry on falling to pieces you can't distinguish the connection between words and you fall confusedly asleep

Later the sun rises and it all starts over again.

Migmar and Lu Gao had some risky adventures in the few days we were there.

"After lunch Teacher Lu and I went out over the bridge. The other side of the bridge is the old quarter of Burang, where there are some very dilapidated mud-brick houses. We saw that there were several caves at the top of the cliff and climbed up, it was a very steep slope. On the way up we saw an eagle's nest, very shallow with a pair of just hatched eagle chicks, we didn't touch them. It's all wind eroded rock and the white arrow-shaped traces of eagles claws could be seen everywhere.

"Eagles were flying to and fro overhead, sometimes practically ruffling my hair, they flew really low. Looking at Burang from the top of the cliff was really interesting. It was like a large crater that had just been formed by an earthquake and was filled with pebbles large and small. The large were higher than houses and the small mud huts nestled invisibly within the huge stones, you could just see people moving about in the cracks between the stones. They looked as small as ants.

"Later we climbed to the foot of a cave. The mouth wasn't large, about shoulder height and you had to bend down to get in. It was dark inside and it took several minutes for your eyes to get used to the darkness. They had been cooking over a wood fire and the walls of the cave were pitch black. The family consisted only of a mother holding a child in her arms, it looked new-born, pink and very small. We went in, the woman took no notice at all. I spoke to her but I couldn't understand a word she said. She was pounding chili peppers in a mortar and taking snuff at the same time. The snuff bottle was made of ox horn, rather nice and the shape not bad."

Little Bai babbles on. Anyhow, you can't get up. Let him say what he wants.

Lu Gao has bought a woven picture in the market. They say that it's handicraft from the people who live in the Nepal, India, Tibet border triangle. Woven in fine wool. The natural color of the wool forms the background and the design is woven in an ochre colored wool thread, judging from the form it's probably some god. Simple and unsophisticated and very tasteful. It's not easy to find this kind of handicraft, even Migmar has never found any. You are filled with envy. Lu Gao is always Lu Gao.

Truth to tell, it's not your daughter and it's not Pedron that you ought to think most about.

You don't admit it? In all conscience! You dare not deny it.

Yes, it's Choegyal.

Little Bai and the merchant remained in Burang.

XX

I cannot deny my conscience. I admit it, I have to think of Choegyal. There's probably no more delicate consideration.

I trudged wearily back, grasping the crane's long withered

legs in my right hand. The feathers below the neck were pure white and the body, stained with fresh blood, trailed on the ground, spattered in mud. I ignored it and dragged soullessly back to camp. I walked neither fast nor slow, mechanically, with dulled senses. An insensate animal. Not just one, there's more.

I walked back like this, I even closed my eyes. My stride did not alter—my pace did not alter—my pulse did not alter. Indeed, I didn't even feel tired.

I heard laughter but was reluctant to open my eyes, it was the sound of Pedron and Princess. I arrived and stood there with my eyes still closed. My right hand opened and the legs of the crane fell to the ground. Because the shoulder drooped, the gun over my left shoulder slid slowly down from the shoulder; the sling slipping from shoulder to elbow to the back of the hand, the gun hitting the ground with a feeble sound.

I stood for a moment and then dragged myself into the tent.

Little Bai was awake, looking at me lifelessly. Lying there motionless.

Lu Gao was busy with the fish that lay gutted and drying on the gravel.

Princess was holding Little Bai's *Philosophy of Art* in both hands with Pedron close to her. I didn't feel like staying in the stuffy tent or feel like striking up a conversation with Little Bai and just walked out to the two women sitting in the sun.

Their interest obviously lay in some artistic engravings containing naked women. Princess looked up at me, happily showing her teeth and laughing. Unlike the average girl in the interior she showed an unrestrained interest in the naked body and did not, because of the presence of a male hastily turn the page. Her utterly open attitude emphasized her purity. There was no doubt that this was the first time that they had seen this kind of illustration. Princess looked up and smiled at me again, I was baffled. This time she was by no means so pure.

Pedron looked up as well, glanced at me quickly and lowered her head. She cautiously extended the index finger of her right hand and gently rubbed it over the naked body of the Venus de Milo. Naturally, the surface of the illustration had no contours. I wondered whether or not her mind was the same as the illustration?

They were exchanging experiences, quietly and leisurely, even whispering intimacies. They had definitely forgotten the language barrier. Even if they deliberately raised their voices there was no fear of their intimacies being overheard. None of the three Han understood Tibetan.

Ingres' *The Turkish Bath*, that most famous example of mass nakedness, delighted the two Tibetan women.

I had no interest in talking to them either. I had forgotten the business with Pedron. Forgotten. Forgotten. I strolled aside, lay down on a patch of level sand and pulled my hat over my eyes.

When I opened my eyes the sun was already sinking in the west. I pulled my hat from my eyes and stared at the clear blue sky for a while. There were no clouds and apart from the sun setting over the western horizon there were also two or three large stars. White and utterly clear but not shining at all. The crane had not yet been plucked, there was a lot to do, first boiling water. Plucking needs boiling water, maybe the bitter river water will do. But then there's the water for cooking, need to fetch water and cook when I get back but there's no rice not a grain what's to be done or what's not to be done there's nothing can be done there's no way that Dadra and the others will get back where are they Lu Gao's going to pieces worse luck really worse luck Dadra's got to Burang why didn't I think of Migmar that's right there's still Migmar and the merchant who got a lift there's still Choegyal who hasn't stolen your things merchant I can guarantee that Choegyal hasn't been back it's bound to be One Ear from the sound of it it's bound to be that crafty mate of his and him who knows perhaps One Ear is the female and it's the mate of another it's bound to be them

I wanted to suddenly open my eyes and then all at once remembered that they were already open. I was frightened, the fear seemed completely irrational. No, it was not because of the howling of the wolves; these last few days the sound of the wolves' unceasing howling in my ears had already numbed my senses. I was unwilling to think further; I knew intuitively that the more I thought the more frightened I would be. But why didn't I go out and kill One Ear? And his equally loathsome mate?

One, two, three, up!

Lu Gao was not there, nor was the water can, I reckoned he had probably gone to fetch water. The gun was there and that was good. Little Bai had his eyes closed, I guessed he was pretending to be asleep, he would have heard my footsteps approaching and then closed his eyes. I'll get the gun, never mind him. Then I saw the crane, plucked clean, gutted and kept open with paper just waiting to go into the pot with boiling water. I had certainly slept for a long time.

I thought only of killing those two wolves, I took the gun and several rounds of ammunition. Had Pedron, the two of them, gone?

They were still in the same place, the sun had not yet set. I walked unhurriedly on and as I walked the distance did not seem to decrease. I thought that they had certainly withdrawn as I advanced, but although I watched them all the time they stayed where they were.

Don't go any further, it's useless. Without giving it a thought I raised the gun, aimed—and fired: the smoke cleared and I could no longer see them. The distance was too great, the effective range of a shotgun was less than two thirds of this distance. They were bound to have been frightened off. I knew this quite well, was I just trying to scare them away? I don't know why I fired.

At that moment I felt a faint pain in my lower right abdomen.

XXI

Yao Liang knew that between the merchant and himself there was a bond of affinity.

It must be so, otherwise why was it that Yao Liang discovered Choegyal in the truck that night? And why did the merchant entrust his goods to Yao Liang when they went off to look for a vehicle? Affinity. It was affinity.

Thus, it was only to be expected that when Yao Liang lay between life and death, the merchant should arrive with a vehicle in the nick of time. Isn't that so?

Yao Liang very much regretted that although they had been together for so long, he didn't know the merchant's name. Behind his back they all called him "merchant." Nobody greeted him face to face, he was the passenger. Dadra didn't know what his name was. Yao Liang suspected that perhaps Dadra didn't know him and had, for a sum or for goods, agreed to take him as a passenger. In Tibet, the drivers often used this as a way of earning a little cash on the side.

As far as could be seen the relationship between the merchant and Dadra was not particularly harmonious. On the road Dadra paid little attention to the merchant who appeared completely unconcerned. So that when the three of them went looking for a vehicle and came to the first crossroads, Dadra detached the merchant.

"It's like this," said Dadra. Of the three of them he was the obvious leader. "We'll separate, if we separate there's a greater possibility of finding a vehicle. Migmar and I will go this way and you go that way, all right?"

"Right." What else could the merchant say?

Dadra was a driver and quite good at distinguishing one road from another. The road that he and Migmar took was a main road, in fact the national road that they had been following. Although vehicle tracks were not obvious there was still a road bed that could be followed. As long as nothing happened and they carried straight on, this was obviously the way to rescue. As for the other road? If something really happened to the merchant, Yao Liang would never forgive Dadra.

Fortunately, the merchant was Tibetan. They were better

able to cope with a harsh environment; had it been Yao Liang there is no doubt that he would have died. The road he had taken veered northwards, that taken by Dadra lay westwards.

It is wrong to say that this vast area is uninhabited; there are a few scattered herdsman and hunters, they raise livestock on small patches of grassland and exist tenaciously in an extremely harsh environment. It's just that because of the sparse population in this vastness, the newcomer is given the impression of an untouched primitivism. Very rarely do the inhabitants here congregate in villages. Because there are no extensive areas of grassland the congregation of large numbers of people in one place would cause difficulties for the raising of livestock. They mostly occupy a single or several strips of grassland as individual families and raise a few yaks and some sheep, a couple of tents and three to five people is the commonest form of settlement here. Some also have sheep dogs.

Dadra and Migmar hadn't gone far when they met just such a family. They were able to merrily drink tea with milk, sleep well for a while and return to the road strengthened and refreshed. At night they could lodge with a herdsman; they could ask their host about conditions and how far they would have to go before they met anybody else. Sometimes, when they knew that it would be a whole day's journey before they met anybody, they had to stopover early and set out very early the following day.

Stopping and starting like this they had walked for six whole days by the time they reached Burang. When you reckon it up, an average of over 50 *li* a day is quite arduous. Once there, they didn't stop to rest but immediately set about arranging a vehicle. Finding a vehicle was not difficult, the difficulty was fuel. A single vehicle there and back would take three days at the least and would require at least 100 liters of gasoline. Gasoline was tight and depended upon supply from outside. Dadra and Migmar discussed this fruitlessly and reached no solution. They went to the local authorities, the county head promised to find a way and asked them to wait two or three days.

"But, perhaps they'll soon be dead ..." Migmar said tearfully.

The county head genuinely wished to help and had not spoken out of mere politeness. Don't make excessive demands. In the end, however, the county head couldn't help them because Lu Gao and the others had already arrived in Burang.

After the merchant had parted from Dadra and Migmar, he set off alone and completely unaided into the wilderness.

He walked for the rest of the day, even eating on the march. This was probably because his goods were on the vehicle and so he was keener than others on rescue. He met nobody; the road had left the path of the river, so there was no water. He eat a tin of pineapples.

The night was cloudy, sometimes overcast and sometimes clear. He didn't rashly press on. He didn't want to get lost. The vehicle tracks on this road seemed fresher than those on the road that Dadra had taken; it seemed to, be a new route used by a convoy of vehicles, because there was no actual road bed. There seemed to be no loose earth on the surface and the ground was firm. Despite the fact that the convoy had passed through some time ago, the vehicle tracks could still easily be made out.

He lay down beside the road clasping his bag. To guard against all eventualities, he drew his long-hafted Tibetan sword from its scabbard and grasped it in his hand.

He slept very well that night. No wild animals disturbed him. He woke when it was light and set out without delay.

As he recalled, he travelled furthest the second day because he still had the energy and the food as well. He had five tins in all, two meat and three fruit. He came across nobody that day and his tins were reduced to two.

The road looked rather unreliable, otherwise why were there no people living along it? Moreover, there were no large stretches of grassland and even very few animals. The outline of hills appeared in the distance. The road was no longer level but went slowly uphill and downhill.

When it was dark he met a small herd of gazelle, about five or six of them. For Tibetans killing gazelle was not taking life, it was much the same as slaughtering livestock you had reared. But the merchant had no gun and could only watch impatiently as they went by.

The tin of meat that he had eaten in the middle of the day had long since been digested by the lengthy journey. He was hungry but knew that there was only one tin of pork left and so held back. He slept as soon as it was dark to avoid his stomach rumbling when he was even hungrier. It was difficult to sleep.

Something happened that night.

He slept heavily but now and then felt as if his face and neck were being tickled. He shook his head impatiently but still couldn't get rid of it. He wasn't dreaming. If he had been he might perhaps have seen his son (if he had one) mischievously playing with him. He had to open his eyes.

The sky was of an unparalleled clarity. The careful reader will realize that this was the night that Yao Liang recorded snowfall in his diary. It was not the same here, apart from a sky filled with shining stars there was the crescent of a first quarter moon. This was not, of course, the first thing that the merchant saw. It was the leopard. The silhouette of the leopard stood out very distinctly against the background of stars. It had just been licking him with its long tongue.

The leopard was sniffing at him. Was he frightened or not? Or so immediately frightened that his trousers were completely soaked? Of one thing we can be sure, he didn't move. Not an inch. Perhaps this was the decisive factor that made the leopard let him go.

It went—nonchalantly.

Thank heavens.

This is not something that every one of us will encounter. It seems to have little to do with words like bravery or courage. When it happens, that is the way of it: and when it does, it will have a full stomach (perhaps). It was fate, he couldn't go back to sleep. Open your eyes and count the stars.

By the third day he had eaten all his supplies and had still met nobody. There was nobody on the fourth day. He had no more strength and just drank a little water. There was no way that he could carry water with him.

He didn't sleep the fourth night, perhaps because he felt that if he did he would never wake up. No, perhaps because he had a premonition that his journey would soon end.

At a certain moment in the morning he felt utterly exhausted and decided to sit and rest for a while, for ten minutes, or for an hour. As a result he slept, slept through to the Western Paradise.

He was discovered and brought back by a geological unit. She was a woman in her forties from Henan hired as a cook for the geologists, she was also the wife of one of the members of the unit, Old Zhang, everybody called her Sister Zhang. She cooked a hot thick porridge and called the merchant to eat. Surprisingly, he woke as soon as called.

He was only faint with hunger and just hadn't slept for a night. After five hours of heavy sleep and several large bowls of piping hot congee he was a man once more. He told the story of the trapped truck.

Like a fire engine to a fire, the unit leader dispatched a tow truck with two drivers who drove non-stop in turns and at noon on the sixth day they reached the crossroads where the merchant had separated from Dadra. Try as he might he couldn't think which direction to take.

Based on the driver's analysis, they decided to turn left. As a result they drove until it was dark without finding the trapped vehicle. Strangely, they came to another T-junction, there are three witnesses who can swear to it. They turned round again.

Master Hu, the Han driver from the Northeast said they were back where they'd started and once in this situation they wouldn't get out whatever they did. It was not the first time that Phuntsok had experienced this sort of situation either.

They decided to stop and leave it until the next day. Damnable northeastern superstition.

Finally, Lu Gao's hoped for vehicle arrived but he couldn't see either Dadra or Migmar. Sitting in the driving cab with the driver and the merchant was a young Tibetan, the driver wasn't Dadra.

The merchant introduced them. "This is Master Hu, this is Master Phuntsok, this is Teacher Lu. Where are Teacher Yao and the other?" Lu Gao told him that Yao Liang and Little Bai were in the tent.

XXII

You crouched down but the pain in your abdomen was even worse. You tried pressing gently. It was impossible. The slightest touch and the pain was unendurable.

Then you simply sat on the ground and let your abdomen expand, that seemed a little better. It certainly wasn't a coronary, the heart couldn't extend into the right-hand side of the abdomen. Lean back and to the right.

The sky darkened. Moments ago, the sunset sky had just been grey-blue with a hint of transparency; now the greyish tone grew second by second and quickly swallowed the remaining blue. The sense of transparency also vanished.

Your elbows touched the ground, half lying, half crouching. You prayed that the pain would quickly recede. Perhaps you didn't hope at all, at the time all your senses were dulled and numb.

Perhaps it was appendicitis?

No strenuous exercise after meals had been the idea when you were young, it lead to appendicitis they said. Of course you didn't understand medicine or its principles. Besides, you hadn't eaten and hadn't taken strenuous exercise. The gun was beside you, you could stretch out a hand and reach it. Perhaps they realized that something had happened to you and would reappear, they were spirits. You believed that there was nothing that they did not know. Then let them come if they wanted.

Moreover you knew absolutely that they would come. As you thought of this your nerves were keyed up. Perhaps you made an effort to open wide your bulging eyes like somebody suffering from mental illness.

Is it still painful?

Tired out and with aching eyes your sight becomes blurred. But you will not accept that you are delirious.

You see a leopard. Not the frequently seen snow leopard. Snow leopards are white. A dirty white splashed with mud.

It is the color of gleaming gold, as graceful and magnificent as an aristocratic lady, or perhaps more like an expensive prostitute. It shimmers with a blazing sensuality, it's movements deliberate and elegant. You conclude at once that it is a female.

Almost at the same time you see the merchant. He is lying on his side beneath the night sky, wrapped up and asleep, his leather Tibetan robe already damp in the night frost. That lascivious creature, its whole body stitched in black coin-like patches, stalks up and the patches overshadow the merchant.

It's regrettable that you only—you didn't see that One Ear and his mate were already there, in front of you. The blue of the sky became deeper and deeper, so deep that it was no longer transparent. Appendicitis? No.

Perhaps you didn't want to know how the merchant reacted, but you certainly thought of it, many animals (including man—male and female) have wonderful experiences. Sex should be a universal rule and there should be no great distinction between man and animals. Suffering is a wonderful experience as well. It really hurts.

When authors write about sex, it's full of ambiguous suggestion. You know that your vision of the merchant is a fabrication. The merchant, Dadra and Migmar have gone to find a vehicle. Then, who is he? And who is the golden leopard?

Oh! Balzac! Oh! That great book *A Passion in the Desert*!

It can't be anything else but a book, a romantic story.

But why do you look at me like that? You're laughable. Laughable! I hate you both, especially you! Why are you so funny? With just one ear? Swaying from side to side in that self-satisfied way? It really hurts.

What are you thinking? You ask it with a look.

What do you say? Go on tell me. F--k off! I don't want you, I don't want you looking at me and I don't want to know what you're thinking. I hate you, you swaying One Ear, with that pre-meditated look on your face. Come on, come on, come on! It really hurts. What can it be?

You cannot pick up the gun and you don't really care what they do to you. Let them do what they want.

I'm in pain; that's what you decided.

You certainly lost consciousness, slept or ... were in shock. Otherwise you would have known how you were discovered by the two women and carried back. You didn't know. You only found out later.

Perhaps Pedron and Princess have both forgotten what they were doing but they discovered you and carried you back to the tent—this was the only thing they did. It was Pedron, and affinity.

It was dark then, Lu Gao came back from fetching water, saw that you were not there and that only Little Bai was in the tent. Lu Gao cupped his hands into a trumpet and called your name loudly. You didn't know this of course. Lu Gao went outside, blundered about and after a while blundered into Pedron and Princess.

After all the gesturing, they both completely understood and the three of them went in three different directions. Pedron, walking in haste, tripped over your recumbent body. Ah, Pedron, Pedron, what can one say?

Lu Gao told you later that when Pedron tripped and found that it was you she burst out wailing, she didn't help you up let alone touch you, she was over-joyed. It was her wailing that attracted Princess and attracted Lu Gao too who had already walked some distance. By the time Lu Gao arrived, the two women had already carried you back towards the tent.

You didn't move, just breathed shallowly but Little Bai was awake and tried to get up. He was firmly pushed back down by Princess. Pedron, was no longer noisy, but continued to sob quietly.

XXIII

At this point I must make a statement, a solemn one.

This novel by Mr. Ma Yuan is utter bloody nonsense. A certain Somebody Yao has become his puppet. All the misfortune has been my lot, it's not right.

First, the wound on my stomach is the scar from an operation for appendicitis when I was six and a half, he has exploited it to make up this puzzling story. There's not a shadow of truth in it, he just took advantage of it for his own ends.

Next, a real man keeps what can't be said to himself. You say that I'm affectionate, that I'm a little man, I'm not bothered; but Yao Liang is not a character who is always trying to get into women's knickers, I have never indulged in seduction. Look, it was me, a certain Somebody Yao and Little Bai that did the womanizing, we were the two who ended up injured and ill! Lu Gao gained a cheap advantage and is showing off.

(Let me whisper you a little behind the scenes gossip—Lu Gao is actually Ma Yuan. He's a fellow all prettified up for himself.)

The third problem is very substantial,

Mr. Ma Yuan himself has never been to the uninhabited western region of Tibet, I'll swear that on my life. All the details are inaccurate. Consequently, he plays tricks with the form of the novel, deliberately sowing confusion in order to achieve an effect, so that the reader can't separate truth from falsehood. Just think it over.

Names. The forms of address, you, I, and he spin round like a revolving lantern so that the point of view of the speaker fluctuates the whole time and the reader's sense of coherence and continuity is disturbed.

Double-track description. This is a sly trick which lets you obscure situations that you can't handle. Breaking off and re-joining. This allows you to ingeniously evade the original point of cut off and use a re-join in a new form as a poor substitute. Like keeping away from the main enemy and attacking his points of weakness.

Subject matter. Using sexual content in the very lowest way to adjust the balance because you fear that the fictional bits lack a sense of reality and would fail to interest the reader. Sex turned out to be pepper which resulted in a great deal of trouble for me, what was the point of being bloody ruined by him?

(Dear reader—you are bound to want to know why Mr. Ma has allowed me to insert this passage into his novel. I can tell you—it's no great secret—it's because of an agreement we had. That if he wanted to publish the novel, the statement went with it, otherwise I would sue him. He was unwilling to be sued and so this statement has been published along with the novel. In fact he doesn't realize that publishing this statement is the equivalent of suing him in the court of public opinion, in the end he's going to fall into my hands. I am certain that you will be on my side. Thank you.)

XXIV

Stories must be told to the end and novels must have a conclusion.

Yao Liang says that nothing matters. What he has to say on this matter doesn't count—he should know this. Alas, he doesn't.

I am fascinated by the number 24. I know that I must finish in this chapter. Yao Liang occupied a chapter to himself, otherwise I might perhaps have developed the story further in that chapter. Yao Liang is lovable but after the calamity he has experienced, his mind has been upset. There are things that he can no longer remember clearly. He often speaks incoherently and mixes up utterly unconnected events, after all, he underwent that unimaginable operation under very unfavorable conditions. The fact that he survived at all was luck in the midst of misfortune.

To tell the truth, Yao Liang was quite right—I never went to the uninhabited region and of course I never had the pleasure of witnessing such a legendary operation. I'm not Lu Gao, that goes without saying.

In order to write the conclusion to this novel I must take a look at the related literature on surgery. It so happens that a second-hand bookshop contained a very appropriate example called *Compendium of Materials on Surgical Operations Performed During the Soviet Union's War of National Defense 1941–1942.* It was reduced, originally 7.50 yuan, now reduced by 30%. Too expensive.

I decided to save myself 5.25 yuan and conjure up something from my own imagination, I thought it would probably do. Although surgical operations involve a detailed technical process, I was full of confidence. Fabrication is my talent. That's the way it is, on this point there's no way I can be modest (nor does there seem to be any use for modesty), right?

There should be an accounting as to the characters, a complete accounting.

The merchant's account is complete. Little Bai's story concluded when he was gored by the wild yak. The story of Lu Gao has yet to bear fruit and may never do so, and will probably carry on being told over the next few decades.

The big difficulty is Dadra and Migmar.

There are no great peaks and troughs in the characters of these two, they are not characters who grow and change, they are on stage too little and there is even less dramatic conflict. To be modest, it could be said that this was due to lack of literary ability; a less than modest cunning might suggest that it was not impossible that they were like this anyhow. Dadra is no fool. He was much moved by the concern shown for him by Lu Gao and Yao Liang when he caught a cold from bathing in the lake. However, he is not the sort of man to go spouting his thanks. He will use his own or the Tibetan way of expressing it at a suitable time. That's something for later.

There is no doubt that in the end, Yao Liang is the victim. No wonder his anger could set the very air on fire. His performance is not over.

There is still a small tail of a role for the two women.

Going through all the characters from start to finish just leaves Choegyal. If it was not for the fact that he finally appears in person, he would still be rather enigmatic. However, neither Lu Gao nor Yao Liang ever worked out what sort of person Choegyal was.

Logically, he should not be here, particularly since it was already dark. One possibility is that Pedron went back and told him. Princess stayed in the tent to help Lu Gao and Little Bai. If somebody went to call him, it couldn't have been Princess. Nobody remembers what Pedron was doing at the time, perhaps it was her, we should consider the fact that she had the most concern for Yao Liang's life.

There is another possibility.

Choegyal was anxious lest the two women had met with an accident and arrived here during the process of looking for them. Or, was he thinking that he could come by more ill-gotten wealth from the truck?

What is important is that he came, we can ignore the reasons and motivation for his arrival, it's the actual fact of his arrival that is crucial.

He asked Lu Gao: "What's the matter?"

Lu Gao turned and looked at Choegyal, and shook his head with a numbed expression.

"What's wrong with him?"

"I don't know."

"Let me see," Choegyal knelt.

With the thick thumb of his right hand he pressed down on the acupuncture point in the middle of the upper lip, heavily, and again, heavily. During that seven or eight minutes the corners of Yao Liang's mouth twitched and he calmly opened his eyes.

Yao Liang did not want to talk, his eyes opened for a while and then closed. This time however, there was no shock. His right hand moved and slowly but without effort extended to his right abdomen.

His brow twitched subconsciously. And again.

Choegyal undid Yao Liang's belt, pulled aside his underclothes and tucked down his underpants. He then gently felt the painful spot.

Without any attempt at avoiding suspicion the two women crowded attentively round.

Choegyal looked as if he had had a great deal of experience, his fingers lightly rising and falling while he concentrated on observing Yao Liang's reactions. He then took Yao Liang's left hand and examined the lines on the palm like a palmist. Finally, he took hold of Yao Liang's chin, opened the jaw and looked inside.

Choegyal turned and looked up, Lu Gao was looking at him. Their eyes met for some seconds. Choegyal spoke in a level, low voice: "It's appendicitis."

Pedron hurriedly interjected a phrase and Choegyal responded instantly. At once, Pedron's face took on an expression of alarm.

Lu Gao asked Choegyal: "What did she say?"

"She asked whether he could die, I said he might."

"Can anything be done?"

Lu Gao's tone of voice had changed.

Choegyal did not respond at once. After a while he said: "It'll have to be cut out."

He paused for a moment and then added: "Otherwise, he's done for."

Lu Gao strode rapidly back and forth with long paces. He suddenly turned to Choegyal: "Are you a doctor?"

"I studied veterinary science."

More pacing, and then a standstill.

In the tent it was as quiet as death.

More pacing but the tempo was clearly slower.

Halt.

Choegyal turned and looked at Lu Gao.

Lu Gao looked hard at Choegyal for over ten minutes. In all this time Choegyal did not blink.

"Choegyal," there was a fierceness in Lu Gao's tone.

"Choegyal, do it, I'm handing him over to you."

He turned and left the tent, the rifle in his hand.

Choegyal told the two women to boil water and extracted the bandages, alcohol and cotton wool balls from the first-aid kit. With a pair of surgical scissors he clipped smooth Yao Liang's pubic hair. The water had not boiled.

Choegyal also went outside.

The night sky was clear. A bright halo surrounded the half-moon which robbed the stars of their light. Choegyal quickened his step.

Half an hour later, he returned to the tent with a fully grown sheep over his shoulder. Pedron was a natural wife, her husband's helpmate. Without a word, she picked up the pressure lamp and held it so as to give Choegyal light.

Choegyal deftly slaughtered the sheep, opened the abdomen, removed the small intestine and with bloody hands cut it into strips of uneven thickness to make surgical thread.

He called to Lu Gao. Lu Gao was nowhere near.

Lu Gao—Lu—Gao—Lu Gao—

Lu Gao answered and rushed back. Panting, he asked Choegyal: "What, what do you want me for?"

"There are two doses of Procaine."

"What for?"

"As an anesthetic, I don't think just a local anesthetic will do, I'm afraid he may not be able to stand it. I think," he paused.

"Think what?"

"I think you should help me tie him up."

Lu Gao and Choegyal turned Yao Liang on his side, found a length of squared timber about 2.5 meters long and several lengths of thin rope and bound him firmly down on the timber. Yao Liang seemed too weak to struggle and even lacked the will to show an interest.

Lu Gao eventually left.

Choegyal found a syringe, swabbed it with a cotton wool ball a couple of times, broke the seal on the phial, pushed the needle deep in and drew up the medicine into the syringe. Combining the two doses he injected them into a spot in the right abdomen where the tissue was comparatively thick.

The water in the pressure cooker began to boil.

Choegyal drew the knife that hung at his waist. He had just used it to slaughter the sheep, the back of the blade was still stained with blood and in the glare of the pressure lamp reflected a cold light. He grasped the haft of the knife and plunged the blade into the boiling water. The bubbles immediately subsided. At once, tendrils of red radiated from the blade but this sight lasted only for a moment, the bubbling resumed and the clear water changed to a muddy white. The water boiled up again.

Pedron looked nervous as Choegyal withdrew the knife from the water. She watched the blade and watched Choegyal's every movement.

Choegyal lifted the knife to his eyes and examined the blade carefully. He was waiting for the knife to cool. The blade was keen and light. Altogether a fine knife.

All the while, Princess stood watch at Little Bai's side, clinging to one of his hands, now and then looking at Choegyal and then looking down at Little Bai. Little Bai was looking at Choegyal too.

Apart from the slight sound of shallow breathing Yao Liang did not show any sign of life.

Choegyal moved in between Little Bai and Yao Liang; his broad back casting an enormous shadow that completely covered Little Bai. Little Bai knew that he was deliberately preventing him from seeing the operation. The pupils of Little Bai's eyes expanded and then suddenly closed.

Pedron picked up the pressure lamp and found the best position for illumination. She didn't move until Choegyal gestured to her.

It began.

Holding the haft of the knife in reverse like a pencil, Choegyal made a firm incision in Yao Liang's belly. Yao Liang cried out. The sound was filled with unendurable anguish, dark and despairing.

Following the movement of the blade, a layer of white body fat tissue opened like a pair of lips and drops of fresh blood appeared. This time it was Pedron's turn to groan.

Choegyal did not raise his head but swore vigorously in Tibetan. Pedron immediately choked back her groaning.

Choegyal's heavy breathing was the only sound in the tent. Yao Liang no longer cried out, probably through shock. The incision was large and the operation continued for a long time.

Little Bai tried hard not to open his eyes. In the end he was unable to bear it, but fortunately when he did open them,

Choegyal was stitching up. He saw that Choegyal's hands and Yao Liang's belly were stained with blood.

Choegyal stood up and emitted a long sigh. He looked exhausted. Little Bai saw him pick up the dead sheep and realized that he was about to go. Choegyal looked up at the sky and turned to Little Bai.

"I don't know his blood group so there can't be a transfusion. But I used musk so there probably won't be any infection. He'll live."

He slung the dead sheep over his shoulder and left.

It was getting light. The two women stood guard over the two recumbent men. The men closed their eyes. The women began to drowse.

Suddenly there was a gunshot, two shots, one after the other. The early dawn air vibrated. Yao Liang, who had been unconscious since that first cry at the beginning of the operation, woke up. Little Bai woke. Princess ceased to drowse and clutched fiercely at Little Bai. Pedron stood and went out. The sky was bathed in the pink glimmer of dawn.

Pedron sighed gently.

Lu Gao had returned.

He dragged in a leopard. A real golden leopard, its fur a shimmering golden yellow, with a quivering deep black coin pattern. He took out his knife and without a word set to skinning the leopard. The skinned pelt was flung to the ground. Without resting he opened the abdominal cavity, removed the inner organs and tossed them aside, taking the heart and the blue green gall bladder and chopping the remainder of the carcass into several large pieces. By now the sun was high.

Lu Gao had not told the women to do anything, he heated the water to rinse the pan and crushed the large bones with a heavy weight. Throughout the whole process he said nothing and looked at nobody, while the remaining four of them gazed at him.

He cut the soft quivering heart into thin slices and boiled them quickly in the water until the color had just changed to white, took the pan off the fire, added a little salt, filled two bowls and served them to Little Bai and Yao Liang.

Too hot. It looked as if Yao Liang had burnt himself badly.

Little Bai blew on it and quickly drank a bowlful.

The two women wanted to go back and Lu Gao gestured to Pedron to take the leopard skin. Pedron indicated that they would come again.

Describing these events has exhausted me. I feel like an executioner, I'm afraid of myself and afraid of this Ma Yuan. I'm afraid that I won't be able to stand it anymore. I'm going to finish it quickly.

There was not much left of the morning. Yao Liang and Little Bai went back to sleep again; Lu Gao cut up the leopard meat and boiled it by himself, this took a long time.

In the morning, no, perhaps it was mid-day, a vehicle arrived. Lu Gao was not excited in the least and watched with complete indifference as the vehicle drive slowly in.

The driver was a middle-aged Han. Next to him was a young Tibetan who seemed to be about the same age as Dadra. The other was the merchant.

The afternoon and evening was spent towing out the truck. Pedron and Princess helped with the cooking. Supper was all leopard meat. Once the truck was hauled out Master Hu suggested that they should go to the geological unit first but Lu Gao thought that they should get to Burang as quickly as possible.

In the end it was decided that Phuntsok should drive the tow-truck back to the unit and that Master Hu should drive Lu Gao's truck to Burang. The two woman didn't go back but remained at the bedside of the two patients. Everybody was tired and there was soon the sound of snoring.

Not a word throughout the night.

In the morning Phuntsok filled the tank of Lu Gao's vehicle and then drove off. Master Hu and Lu Gao carefully loaded the two stretcher cases onto the truck. The merchant opened his bale of quilted robes and laid out brand new quilted garments on the floor of the truck so that Yao Liang and Little Bai could lie a little more comfortably. Finally all the remaining bits and pieces were loaded.

It is the farewells that can be called the real conclusion.

Yao Liang and Little Bai were both awake, they discussed giving Pedron and Princess a little something. But what? Let's see what there is.

An ordinary small round mirror and a ballpoint pen: a plexiglass goldfish decoration; a square, clean handkerchief; and of course, there was also that illustrated copy of the *Philosophy of Art*.

The two bed-bound men smiled at each other. By now Lu Gao had tugged Master Hu off to the driving cab in front. There was a problem over the presents, Princess and Pedron both pointed to a present and then to themselves. It took some time for Yao Liang and Little Bai to realize that they were asking: "Which one is for me?"

They divided them at random. They were really thoughtless and forgot that they were two women and that they, although sick, were two men. Such unforgivable thoughtlessness!

Before Master Hu closed the tailboard, like women of all races the world over, they fiercely kissed their own man. Princess kissed Little Bai, so much so that his face grew red.

Yao Liang responded warmly to Pedron's kisses.

November 1984–May 1985
Lhasa–Shenyang–Beijing

The Master

"In an unfamiliar region it is always necessary for the stranger to begin at once to construct the familiar …"

Graham Greene, *A Burnt-Out Case*

Nothing Already Mentioned Will
Be Raised Again

B usiness isn't bad.

The phrase "little man" ought to be slightly deprecatory. It made its first appearance in 1981 when I wrote the novella *At Kilometer Zero*. In it, the 13 year-old youth Da Yuan says solemnly to the 17-year-old girl Lin Qi: "Elder Sister Qi, may I kiss you?" Lin Qi hugs Da Yuan enthusiastically and says: "You sweetheart! Little man! You are going to be a poet."

Little man is my invention and one day I will apply for a patent. I aspired to write *The Little Men of Lhasa* long ago, the first volume was just bait, tossing a brick to catch jade, wanting to attract people with sensibility to join the ranks of Lhasa's little men. I thought perhaps that this "little" would frighten off a lot of macho males, I was over-anxious. The facts proved it.

The first volume, entitled *A Casual Romance*, was published in the 1986/4 issue of the literary bimonthly *Spring Wind* produced by the Liaoning Publishing House. At this point, I want to introduce some extraneous matter.

The novel had two sections that were independent short story concepts, they were treated as short story structures and were later issued separately. The magazine *Spring Wind* was furious and said that it would look into the manufacturing of two items from a single draft. They would pay no fees in future and so on. Moreover, even before I had put pen to the paper of the novel they deployed hospitality and the promise of large fees to gain control of this short novella, there was no extreme to which they would not go. I had regard for the face of an editorial friend of mine before I accepted hospitality or transferred the rights of my few novellas to *Spring Wind*. *Spring Wind* was published in July and it is now December, I have received no fee and have lost confidence in completing *The Little Men of Lhasa*. According to friends who urged me to take them to court, cases of magazines publishing extracts from complete novels and bits of novellas are a dime a dozen and examples can be found by the score. It seems that the recently announced *National Law on Publishing* has in no way put a stop to this practice. I have decided not to go to court, I've no interest in it, I would only become a news item, a topic of after dinner conversation and a laughing stock. I don't want the money, it will eventually go back to the state, somebody will swallow it whole. There's no point in raising it again.

In continuing to write *The Little Men of Lhasa* I must thank those friends in Lhasa who took the initiative in applying to be little men. There were quite a few of them and it can be said that they replaced the fees owed by *Spring Wind* magazine. In all conscience, how could I brush aside such kindness? There must be authors amongst my readership who will know that the fee for a novella ranges from several hundred to over a thousand yuan. What is a few? Of course, I don't want this money. It was this that I was referring to when I said that business wasn't bad. I must ask the careful reader to forgive me. I talk as I please too much, as if business and writing were both cooked in the same pot, but I do not mean to blaspheme. The Han have always nursed the belief that farming and agriculture were important and that business was to be looked down on, vocabulary to do with business that was originally neutral acquired a pejorative sense. That's enough. Not to be mentioned again.

There is both truth and untruth in the writing of novels, there is a partial truth but the whole is a fiction. Untruth and the principles of aesthetics. Not to be mentioned again.

The title "master" is customarily applied to chess players and artists of great skill. It's borrowed here to describe a Lhasa artist who was willing to be a little man. That's all.

Nothing already mentioned will be raised again. What follows has not been mentioned before.

All right?

Feeling Bad about Oneself

But immediately he said that he was feeling bad about himself, as if having heard that he was about to became famous he would rather be suspected of being a rascal, like the one who burnt down the temple of Athena (What was he called? I can never remember his name) . . .

His misgivings arose because of what I had said previously. I had said that when I wrote I never glossed over anything, if I knew about something, I wrote about it. I used *A Casual Romance* as evidence. His hope of escaping before battle was joined was in vain.

I was absolutely clear about his embarrassing secret. Of course, I could keep my mouth sealed, of course I could put him to one side and write about somebody else. Whatever I did there was no problem. Of course I could gloss over that embarrassing experience and write about the extent of his abilities or the happy ease with which he had achieved his praiseworthy professional achievements.

For him, the fact of living with his wife's family was a dark secret and he was particularly frightened of people conducting a psychological analysis of it. He forgot that he was just an ordinary person, he even forgot that he had himself spoken about the motives for that splendid marriage and that it was to me that he had spoken personally.

Why was it that the master could have no human weakness? (Dialectic.) Should the master be devoid of any flavor of humanity? Were I in his situation, I think the result would probably have been no different.

I, too, knew the value of those painted Buddhist *thangka*. Had that one-eyed woman been willing to be my wife, I would probably have had no hesitation in dragging my own wife to court and clamoring for a divorce. However, there was no possibility of that, she seemed to have loved him to his very toenails, no one else could gain her favor.

The old man was already ill beyond medical aid and sat on his sickbed waiting for death. But drop by drop he created wealth for his worthy son-in-law. He was the greatest *thangka* master since the fifth Dalai Lama and if priced by the foot the value of his creations would outstrip those of Picasso. He had been painting master to the 13th and 14th Dalai Lamas. He was perhaps more than 100 years old.

It was said that his lifetime's production of *thangka* was not less than 30; the 14th Dalai Lama possessed seven, there were a dozen or more scattered amongst the collections of the world's most famous museums and aristocracy or with large art firms or in the hands of a few wealthy property owners. He had a collection of 11 himself and one that he had been painting for a number of years. His eyesight was still good and his arms operated as he wished.

Nobody knew why his daughter was only 30 and he seemed to have no other relatives. It was difficult to imagine how this fossil, more decrepit than history itself, could have produced a daughter. His limbs were fossilizing, the first to lose sense had been his toes and then everything below the ankle had become numb, the flesh and skin dried and stiffened just as the skeleton within completely lacked flexibility.

It was said that he had suffered this illness for nearly half a century. Its symptoms had encroached bit by bit, spreading gradually but inexorably and it was perhaps this that had enabled him to father this one-eyed daughter in time and had prevented him from moving abroad.

He lived in seclusion in a narrow courtyard in the Wapa Ling residential area of Lhasa, where he and his daughter lived, one upstairs and one downstairs. In front of the house, a large willow tree separated his dwelling from the outside world and thus, for a long time, nobody knew that as well as the one-eyed woman, an old man lived there.

Not a hair remained on his head, his bald skull flickered with a reddish light and he had no beard. He seemed tall when he sat up and he appeared a robust old man. The *thangka* painting which he was reputed to have been working on for a number of years was set in in the midst of beautiful embroidery, the four corners braced tightly on the wall opposite. He sat in an attitude of rapt meditation. It was like a barber's chair that could either be adjusted to form a high back-rest or, when he wished to lie down and rest, he could turn a wheel and lower the back-rest so that the chair converted into a sick-bed.

The masterpiece was very nearly complete but his son-in-law estimated on the basis of current progress that (by his own standards of final completion) it would require (or require another) three years or more.

I asked: "Can he live three years?"

"Hard to say."

It seemed that this paragon of longevity rarely received strangers and my visit disturbed the old man. He did not turn to look at me but sat with his arm hanging lifelessly beside the chair, I saw that desiccated hand tremble slightly. I greeted the old man in Tibetan and went round in front of him so that I could observe the graceful bearing of this immortal and also so that I could take a careful look at the yet unfinished picture.

He seemed utterly unconcerned with my greeting, perhaps he was deaf, but I can definitely say that he was not blind, his eyes were electric, though they did not look at me.

He was looking at his painting. At his side, his daughter silently watched over him. Naturally her husband was present, standing behind me and so ill at ease that he seemed another person.

I don't know whether I ought to describe to the reader what

I saw in that picture or how I should accurately communicate what it was that I saw.

The Private Conversation of Males

Of course, he was the real master and not his son-in-law or anybody else. However, it is the son-in-law who is the principal character of this story. The master in this story is this man, the same age as myself.

He had almost no friends. I was his best friend. So I was the only living person he introduced into the room of his father-in-law. I should be proud of that honor.

He was an artist and should know better than I the value of what that old man, in the process of fossilization, was painting, he must really have known, otherwise how could he bear to sleep under the same quilt as that dreadful woman?

Actually, it was I who knew her first. I can't say that she was someone whom people disliked but at the very least she certainly found no favor with men. I was buying a blackstone ring in the Tromsikhang market off the Barkhor. It was very expensive. I really liked it and just as we were about to make a deal and I had my wallet out to pay, the butter market nearby erupted in a riot.

Holding tightly on to my wallet, I stood and watched and saw two men with knives out glaring at one another like two tigers. I didn't know when my wallet left my hand. Only when this one-eyed woman nudged me in the ribs did I discover that it had gone. She gestured towards me with that single snow-white eye and I saw the little pickpocket pushing heavily through the crowd. I quickly followed him out but he was not to be seen. I lost quite a lot of money and I remembered that one-eyed middle-aged woman.

At the time, he was wildly in love with a fellow student from university and said that she had already agreed to come to Lhasa and marry him. She was seven years younger. I had seen her photograph and she looked rather nice. I thought that there was no way that this one-eyed woman could compare with her.

The change was very sudden, he told me that he had already written to her and told her not to come, it was over. He said that it was possible that he would soon be marrying a Tibetan woman. My first reaction was that he was paying a romantic debt, that he had given a Lhasa girl a big belly and had to marry her.

He was a handsome man, not tall but well-built and well proportioned. There was not a hair on his baby-like face, it was as smooth as a mirror. Like many young artists he wore his hair long, he was a tidy man and his hair was fluffy from being washed so often. He was 33 but looked at least ten years younger than I.

The reader knows that the 33 year old one-eyed woman was his fiancé and he took me to the Tromsikhang market to meet her.

"She does her vegetable shopping here every day at this time (about 11 a.m.), she can't be away from home for long. She's agreed to meet you."

We recognized each other immediately. Strangely, neither of us referred to that incident. Shortly afterwards they were married and he moved into her house. I couldn't go to the wedding as I didn't receive an invitation. "We didn't have a ceremony, her father's not well, nobody else was invited either."

"Did you register it?" This was not what I was thinking of.

"Of course. What would be the point of not registering?"

At the time I knew nothing and was even more puzzled. But if he said nothing, I couldn't very well ask.

He and I have a little previous history.

He probably arrived in Lhasa about six months before me, I got off the plane and had just settled into the hotel when he came knocking on the door. He wanted me to play basketball and said that he had heard that a big man had arrived and that he was a basketball player. I said: "Amateur." He said not to be polite and that they were all graduates who had come to Tibet. I said: "Rather an elderly graduate." He asked me how old I was, I said: "Ten years older than you." He smiled and said that it could not be. I said I was 29 and he said: "Do I look 19 to you?" I said: "You can't be more than 22." He asked me which year of the zodiac I was. "Year of the Snake." He shook his head and said: "What a pity! I'm the same age as you." "You must be joking." "It's true." That was four years ago.

He really was the same age as me but my birthday was seven days before his and so I settled comfortably into the role of elder brother. We were also basketball friends.

Where women are concerned, men tend to hold similar views. I can't (for fear of my wife nagging me) talk about mine so I'll describe his. He sometimes came to supper where I lived (that's before my wife arrived in Tibet, he was married not long after she arrived). We both cooked and normally, by the time we had finished eating it was very late. Sometimes he didn't want to go home on his own (saying he feared the solitude that follows an awkward silence) and stayed overnight. My bed was very wide and could accommodate two at a pinch. It was difficult to get much sleep during nights like this and the conversation, which lasted until dawn, was usually about women and sex.

"There's this about women. Their faces may be different but there's not much difference below. I don't care how they look. I like bottoms, the face doesn't matter, Sichuan girls suit my taste, I go for them every time I visit Chengdu, they're cheap too. The cheapest in the whole country. If you want something a little more long-term, then do them a few portraits, done with a little care and they'll never forget you. Ring when you arrive in Chengdu and they'll come at once. They don't necessarily all want cash, it's enough to buy them clothes or a little jewelry, it depends on the length of time."

I said: "I hear that foreigners abhor the idea of men co-habiting with men and women co-habiting with women. But men and women living together is really nothing to speak of. I've a friend who hated collective dormitories and before he graduated wrote a poem—

> It's against the natural order
> For men to live under one roof

And the fact is
That this will soon be over.
What should you say to that?

"There's nothing I can say. Unfortunately."

"I'm told they do the chicken thing—sodomy in the villages in the North-East, that's homosexual love isn't it?" he asked me. I said: "Love, my arse! We've a folk-saying there—*Hua zi* grabs arse, pleasure at last."

"*Hua zi* is somebody's name?"

"No, no, not the name *hua zi*, beggar."

"No love anywhere? Don't they say that that some homosexuals entirely reject the opposite sex? So those buggers don't f--k women?"

"Who knows. Those sort of people mostly have wives and children. Who knows whether they f--k or not. They must, otherwise where would the children come from?"

"This is bloody revolting. I can't imagine what lesbianism is like. Sodomy is enough, but women?"

"This gets worse and worse, let's change the subject."

"It's like this with women. A wife may not be good-looking but she must be virtuous. Lovers on the other hand, the more abandoned the better. That one (meaning his original fellow student) was particularly obedient, she hadn't been infected by the airs of modern womanhood even though she had been at art school for four years. Her paintings weren't that good, no imagination at all. Her basic technique was good, stronger than mine, but actually producing a picture, she was a long way behind."

"Were you going to get married?"

"She wanted to get married and was going to wear a white muslin wedding dress for the ceremony, she'd earned a lot of money illustrating graphic novels, even my western wedding suit had been ordered. It was black, from Baromon of Shanghai, my disheveled appearance really doesn't suit such smart clothes."

"Didn't she mind if you had other women?"

"How could she not care? But she loved me and knew that I loved her too, she reckoned I was just playing around for the moment. Otherwise what? Break off with me? She had some old fashioned views that her mother had taught her—'the loyal minister does not serve two masters, the loyal wife does not marry twice'—her mother was from a literary family and I think her Chinese painting was better than hers."

"She didn't marry you, why should she retain any affection for the rat you are?"

"What difference is there to sleeping with me and marrying me?"

"How many girls are still virgins when they marry these days? On this basis, you've probably already married twenty times."

"I didn't look at it that way, she did. What can you do?"

What can I do?

Naturally, these topics belonged to the time before he was married.

Later, he changed his tune.

"There has to be a return on marriage otherwise there would be no need for that mad rush for the big piece of red paper (the marriage certificate). Isn't a wife just for sleeping with, cooking and having children? Even better if there are no children, it seems she can't have children, she hasn't explained why. She may not look much but she's not bad in bed and good that she can't have children. When you've time I'll take you home to see. See the old man's room upstairs, I guarantee it'll give you a fright, careful you don't bite your tongue off."

This was when I knew that his father-in-law was a living immortal.

"I told her that I wanted to invite you home and she said to let you come. She doesn't talk much, it seems that she has a good impression of you. When can you come?"

"Will it be all right?"

"A feast for the eyes. In this world the old man's *thangka* are unsurpassed, the most expensive was sold for over 30 million US dollars and is in the collection of a Brazilian timber merchant, he's an American with a personal fortune of over 4 billion. He's the richest man in the world."

"I'm afraid of your wife fixing me with that eye of hers. If she looks at me like that it'll make me uncomfortable. It doesn't feel the same being looked at with one eye rather than two."

"You get used to it. To start with I couldn't stand it, later there was a certain charm in being looked at like that. Her style is rather special, quite unlike girls in the interior. To tell you the truth, I couldn't do without her. I'd still want her even if it were not for the sake of her father."

It was all rather mysterious.

The Daily Ledger

His studio was downstairs, adjacent to the living room. There were three rooms downstairs, the other one was used as a kitchen. They were all about the same size, 30 square meters or so. Because of the narrow windows the light was bad and normally the electric light had to be on.

I spent comparatively little time in the studio, mostly because of a power cut. I had intended to take a close look at his current work and the sketches and studies. He could have lit a pressure lamp to help me see, the lamp was beside the door, but he merely said: "No power, no power. Have a look later when there is an opportunity." I never did have an opportunity as I never even had the chance of crossing the threshold of the courtyard again.

I thought that perhaps it was because of those nudes in oil. He liked painting women, especially naked women. Before he was married, studio and living room had been the same. I was not somebody who was taboo so I was the only person who could sit in the room and watch him paint. He had used his own money to hire a model, though usually it was a girl he knew well who would do it for free. There were also some whom I too knew well. When I was there he behaved quite properly with the models, I cannot guess at the situation when I was not there. On the walls of his spacious studio there now hung two nudes, it was rather difficult to see but in outline they seemed to be naked women.

He didn't want me to look closely and I wasn't particularly interested. I had actually thought to myself that his wife may have been the model. I reckoned that, living in his wife's house, he would be unlikely to have girl models, his wife wasn't that old and he would certainly not allow me to see a painting of his wife naked. The small minded measure others by their own standards.

Thinking about myself like this strangely did not injure my self-respect. The two of us were eating together and his wife had gone upstairs to attend to her father. His daily life was so-so, there were no fresh vegetables on the table and the meat was tinned and utterly tasteless.

I thought to ask him, as neither his wife nor father-in-law had any employment, how they managed to live? He said they relied entirely on his salary of 200 yuan a month. This astonished me. My wife and I spent at least 300 a month. It was difficult to conceive how three people could exist on 200 a month.

"In fact, we don't entirely rely on my salary. She has some family savings. I can't make out where the money she spends comes from, perhaps she has a savings account in the interior or rich relatives abroad? She doesn't say and I don't want to know. She always spends her own money when she goes shopping, she's never asked me for a cent. For my part, I make an effort to spend all my salary each month and that's it."

"Don't you send money home to your mother?"

"I do, I just sent 300 at New Year."

"Weren't you married on New Year's Day? How much have you left?"

"173 yuan in all left over from last year, January's salary and heating allowance was 220 and I sent 300 home. The remainder was all spent."

"That's less than 100 left in total, and there's the Spring Festival to come."

"Festival or not, it makes no difference to me. I'm used to hardship."

"Is this what you eat every day?" I pointed to the dishes on the table. He said: "How could we eat tinned food every day? We generally open a tin when there are guests or on Sundays." Good heavens!

I knew that he hardly ever had guests, my visit had caused him expense and I was sincerely ashamed. However I thought at once of a way to put this right. I had a stock of tins at home that I couldn't be bothered to eat; red cooked pork, steamed pork, luncheon meat and all sorts of fatty tins, normally we eat the fruit and vegetable tins first. Lhasa was a city of mountains of tins. I thought that next time I would bring him a load of tins and repay the moral debt that I had incurred.

Unfortunately there was no next time. That is for later.

The weather turned warmer at the end of March and as he had done in previous years he went out sketching with his portfolio on his back. Sometimes to Sunshine Island on the Lhasa River to sketch the Tibetan girls washing colored woolen blankets in the still icy waters of the river; but most of the time he went to the Barkhor to mix with the pilgrims who prostrated themselves full-length to Buddha or the traders who did all kinds of business there.

He often cursed some other fellow students working in Lhasa, saying that if they were looking for a good time they should go to Chengdu and that you shouldn't visit Lhasa for nothing, why bother to waste your time?

He only said this to me and not to their face. He was very concerned for his widowed mother who lived alone and he had applied to come to Lhasa for her sake. When he graduated it was impossible for him to have been posted to Beijing and he had decided to achieve his aim by roundabout means. According to state regulations, intellectuals posted back to the interior from Tibet were always posted to their original place of residence, the fact of his mother living in Beijing was the be all and end all of being posted back there.

He worked furiously. He produced more paintings than the three fellow students who came with him put together. In this respect he could be called a model for all the graduates who had come to Tibet.

I have to say that his innate artistic talent was a little lacking, what deserved respect was his subsequent effort. He believed deeply in that encouraging idea of genius acquired through hard work. It was modest of him to say that the basic technique of the girl fellow student seven years his younger who had bought his wedding suit for him was better than his own, it was immodest to have said it in order to demonstrate that he was a man with heaven sent creative ability.

All the above is like keeping a daily ledger. I know more clearly than the reader that if it goes on like this, this novel is doomed to failure.

A change of method then.

Suspense to the Fore

He came to see me the morning of the day before this fatality occurred. At the time, I was waiting at the hospital on account of another fatality and my wife asked him in to wait for me, she then went off to work.

He turned over an old draft of mine on the desk and fell asleep as he read it. It was my wife who woke him when she came back from work. He rubbed his bleary eyes and was embarrassed.

Later, my wife told me that she had told him that I probably wouldn't be back for supper. I had rung her in the afternoon to say that I was at the hospital and that Thondup had been hit by a Mitsubishi SUV, the doctor had said that there was perhaps some hope, I would wait to see what happened.

He hesitated over going back. He probably thought it over and felt that he still wanted to see me and had gone to the hospital. By then, Thondup had died and I had naturally left the hospital.

He had obviously learned accurate news of Thondup's move to the mortuary before knocking at my courtyard gate again. This time it was not in vain, it was approaching one o'clock in the morning.

I was not asleep but my wife was already in bed. Fortunately, we had two rooms and where my wife was lying down was the inner bedroom, because of this he didn't quite know whether to sit or stand and said that he had "disturbed" us.

I should say that at the time I was completely enveloped in my own misery. I paid no attention to whether or not he had disturbed my wife and of course I overlooked his appearance of extreme unease. I cared only about the sudden death of Thondup.

He obviously sensed my feelings. He was like a puppet on a string speaking a script. This one man show should have been performed by me alone, his intervention transformed a great tragedy into a comedy double act.

More than I, he was concerned about the detail of how Thondup met his death and he was filled with interest in the whole process whereby Thondup had finally come to be mobilized by me from the Sangdun grasslands to Lhasa. He said he was the earliest reader of my short story about Thondup called *Song of the West*. He said that he had had a colored illustration in the same issue of the magazine and when he had visited the printers to check the color, by coincidence he had seen the original draft of *Song of the West* set in type, it was the first time he had seen my name. "It made a deep impression." Not the novel, just the sight of the name.

"So I remembered you and the famous Gesar bard. Didn't Thondup have a younger brother called Donyo who joined the army and later died, isn't that right?" Actor's lines.

"You wanted to make this story into a graphic novel with 120 illustrations, the largest would fill a thirty foot canvas, and put all the Sangdun grasslands in the story. You said that when Thondup came to Lhasa you would definitely visit him. Now he's come and immediately left again. There was no affinity between the two of you, none!" I burst into tears as I spoke, careless of the fact that my wife was asleep and would have to go to work early next morning.

"I had just heard that you had gone to the Sangdun grasslands to meet Thondup and bring him back to Lhasa. If I had known a little earlier (before you left) I would have taken a trip to the Sangdun grasslands with you, I hear your vehicle reached Lhasa this morning, is that right?" Actor's lines.

"It's my fault. It's my fault! We had crossed the bridge over the Lhasa River into the city when he said that he wanted to relieve himself, the vehicle stopped and he urinated against a wall on the left-hand side of the road. He turned and ran back towards where the vehicle was parked but looked neither left nor right as he crossed the road and was knocked down by a green and black Mitsubishi. The Mitsubishi made an ear-piercing sound as it braked and we (a comrade from the Office for the Rescue of the *Epic of King Gesar*, the driver and I) were in time to see his body crushed to a bloody pulp with our own eyes. We had no time for preserving the scene or arguing the toss with the Mitsubishi's driver or even noting down its registration number but picked up Thondup's bloodied body in our Jeep and rushed him to the hospital's operating theatre. What more do you want to hear?"

"Did the Mitsubishi drive towards your Jeep head on?" Actor's lines.

"I can't remember. We were in the driving cab, we saw it all—yes, it was head on, otherwise how could we have seen it all—so clearly?"

"Don't you believe in fate? Isn't this fate? He could only live in the Sangdun grassland that nurtured him and sing for its herdsmen and its eagles and sheep and for its glorious skies. You made a mistake in dragging him to Lhasa to force him to make recordings of his songs. It was you who did him harm, isn't that fate?"

In the event, he did not say why he had come looking for me in the middle of the night. There was not the opportunity. Nor did I think to ask him why he wanted to see me.

I vaguely remember him talking about something else. The

conversation I have recorded above is totally from memory and I cannot vouch for its complete accuracy, in fact I should not have surrounded it with those damnable quotation marks.

I remember he seemed to have said something about a murder plot. If you asked me to remember the moment, I would definitely confirm that he said that there might be people who wanted to murder Thondup, because at the time I could think of nothing else but Thondup. But now my recollection is definitely guiding me more and more in the direction of the intended victim not being Thondup but ... it's no good, I can't tell you. I remember that in the title of this chapter I warned you and warned myself: suspense to the fore!

The Yellow Notebook

Like a private detective I have compiled a dossier of this case. I have strenuously recalled all the people and events connected with it and visited very many places to try and clarify some of its tangled problems. That's being a detective for you.

I went first to the ruins of the famous Ganden Monastery with an enlarged color photo of him and visited many lay people and monks engaged in its restoration. Contrary to my expectations many of them recognized him or remembered him. I noted down what they said, in all its detail, in a yellow notebook. There were children who showed me objects that had belonged to him and I carefully took photographs of them. He had also visited the ruins of other temples and had spent a long time with the peasants and herdsmen of the neighborhood.

Of course, you can imagine that his footprints covered the whole of Tibet, he would never neglect any temple or monastery that could be visited, however large or small. He was extremely assiduous and would spend eight months of the year backwards and forwards between several thousand Buddhist temples. He travelled less after he was married.

He was one of the few artists who had visited the ruins of the kingdom of Guge, he went by himself, hitching rides in conditions of considerable hunger and hardship. Before he went, he bought a large number of pencil torches and pairs of army boots. These articles ended up in the hands of nomadic herdsmen in the uninhabited region who discarded them after use, I found some and brought them back. On the basis of these objects I can make a guess at all his experiences of this trip of his to Ali. Ali is the Tibet of Tibet.

Particularly interesting was my recovery of a Hong Kong made electronic cigarette lighter that I had given him from an altar court at the top of the Guge ruins. The fact that he had lost it in various situations demonstrated his depressing conjuring skills. At the time he thought that he had lost at the altar but there was nothing he could do about it. It was only when he returned to Sengge Tsangpo that he became more certain in his guesswork.

I also saw one of his quick sketches with a family of Tibetan peasants by the Jinsha River. It was a portrait of the matriarch of the family, a woman with beautiful braided hair, she must have been 70 or 80. There was a boy of about two but no men in the family.

I could no longer remember when he had visited the densely populated area of Khamba in Eastern Tibet. But I do remember him talking of Mount Nujiang where he nearly lost his life coming down the mountain, the vehicle overturned but fortunately it was between two large rocks, otherwise everybody would have perished.

At the end of three months at the wheel I had been everywhere that he could have been. The yellow notebook was crammed full and I took myself back to my own summer shaded courtyard on the north bank of the Lhasa River, closed the door and was immediately carried in my imagination back to winter and the December of that miserable death.

Use your brain.

I opened that neither slim nor fat notebook and read from the first page, character by character, line by line, page by page until, after nearly the whole night, I had finished it, all of it.

It seemed to me that this business had been brewing for some time and should have been detected and prevented long ago. That was my first impression.

The pity of it was that, surprisingly, nobody had detected, let alone prevented, something that had such obvious omens. Although I discovered that the outcome could have been foreseen, it would have been difficult for anybody else to have had the opportunity to do so, only I had it. I cannot deny that I was stupid. Admittedly, I could advance numerous reasons for evading the responsibility but I would far rather accept it. Nobody is going to pursue me, the only one doing so is that Han novelist Ma Yuan. I cannot live with myself, it's as simple as that.

His body was discovered very late. It was discovered by a herd boy when it had been rendered shapeless and unrecognizable by the inroads of icy river water. His wife had already made a report to the police many days earlier. After extensive activity without any result the police had given up and sent their papers to file.

It should be said that no one could be certain that it was him. It was an incomplete corpse lacerated by the nibblings of freshwater sturgeon. The flesh that remained on the skeleton floated from the bones and the clothes had long gone. Nobody could say whether he had entered the water unclothed or whether the clothes had been stripped away by fish.

The reader will see that of course, in the end, it was she who identified him. She never wept nor shed a single tear.

It was not the police who called her to identify the corpse. In the beginning the police had not considered that it had any connection with the woman who had made the report so long ago. Furthermore, she arrived at the scene almost at the moment that the police, having received the child's report, were taking charge of the body. The question of space and distance should be clearly emphasized here. The point where the body was discovered was 23 km downstream from Lhasa itself, a willow covered pebble shoal in the Lhasa River. How she got there and at that particular time was a mystery. She identified him from a gold ring that was still on a finger.

The policeman who was standing closest to her said that he heard her call "Oh, Dad" in a low voice. He was rather unsure whether or not this was what she had said, her voice was too soft and he was hesitant and uncertain. However, he was certain that the woman had simultaneously closed her single eye tightly, for about the time it would take to blink three times.

Spring had just arrived.

Out of the Nightmare

Outwardly, his life appeared as it had been before. He still went industriously sketching at the Barkhor and now and then turned aside and came and sat for an hour or two at home with us. He chatted cheerfully. Surprisingly, even my novelist's sensitivity utterly failed to recognize his mental turmoil.

He would not say a word about the death of his father-in-law and naturally we (my wife and I) could hardly mention it. However, in order to guard against all eventualities, I had urged her not exhibit any sign at all of unnecessary concern, I didn't want to arouse his suspicion. The yellow notebook with all his time, (both past and future) did not exist.

Later, he invited me to his studio a number of times, not the studio at his wife's house but the working space allotted to him by his unit. I have to admit that his painting had improved by leaps and bounds.

He still liked painting nudes as he had in the past, from the past to the present without exception all the great masters in oil had been like this and there was no cause for criticism. He said that he almost never went home to paint, he put up a camp bed on the floor of the studio on top of which he placed an old sheepskin and then a cotton mattress, on top of that he put the thick, tattered, dirty quilt from his bachelor days. A dark reddish light glowed from the electric stove at his foot and he switched off the light and used instead the soft light reflected from the stainless steel top of the kettle. We sat on the camp bed drinking tea in silence. Later when I said that I ought to go and said that my wife was frightened of being alone at home, he still wanted me to stay.

I was certain that there was something that he wanted to say to me. He lowered his head and fixed his gaze on the tea bowl on the floor. "I can't bear it. I haven't been back for a long time. A month, perhaps even longer."

I said: "You're painting much better than you used to."

"If you say so."

"Tell me. What were you just about to say?"

"I was going to say that I don't want to go back, I can't bear it! I can't bear it!"

At that last "I can't bear it" the pitch of his voice rose suddenly and I felt intrigued. I was certainly stunned.

"You know I like women. There are people who come here"— he gestured round the room—"every day. Women, models. Then there are those who come who aren't models. All women. Sometimes two at a time, sometimes more, three or four of them. I paint one and the others have to watch in silence from behind me. There are Tibetans and there are Han. I've never painted a Muslim woman, you know, there are quite a few Muslims here in Lhasa, especially traders from Qinghai, Gansu and Ningxia. Where had I got to?"

I said: "I can see that not all of the models in your paintings are Han." He waved a hand to interrupt me: "You can't see. You're an amateur, you can't distinguish the difference between their bodies."

I said: "I think I can. At least in their skin color ..." "Skin color? The more you talk, the more amateurish you get. To the artist's eye, all color is subjective, if I wanted to paint Pushkinova ..." I interjected "Pushkin's wife" to indicate that I knew what he was talking about.

"... with a brown skin, who's to say that it's wrong or out of the question?"

"Of course, nobody's going to pick holes with you over this. There was a black American author who said that Jesus Christ was black, isn't that the same thing? No white Protestants or Roman Catholics hanged him for it."

"For example, what would you say if I put a Tibetan head on the body of a naked Han woman and made the skin color as white as the peak of a young Mount Dangla? How many naked women have you really seen? Apart from those here, I dare say you haven't even seen ten."

I laughed bitterly: "Not more than three."

"That's why I say you basically don't understand women."

"That's true, I don't." I continued to laugh bitterly but in good humor.

"That's enough, let's not talk about women any more. You must go straight home to bed with your wife, too much talking about women sticks in your throat. Do you dream?"

"Not for a long time, a year, no, probably longer."

"If you've dreamt, you're bound to know the feeling of being trapped in a nightmare. Your whole body is paralyzed, you try to move but cannot, you want to pee but can't get to the lavatory, you can find nothing to use as lavatory paper to wipe your bottom after a shit, you are always seeing half naked women seeming to undress but not, you wet the bed but only feel that your lower body is damp and warm as if you were in a public bath. When you eventually wake up you lie there in a daze for ages, wondering where you are. Much later, you suddenly feel a historically unprecedented sense of relaxation that makes you uncertain of what to do, isn't that it, Big Ma?"

Normally, people close to me call me Big Ma. My surname's Ma (horse) and I'm big, a big horse and a tall man, a large tall horse. Is that a Big Ma?

We talked so much that night that there was no substantial breakthrough in the matter that concerned me. However, never mind, I'm in no hurry and I've no hope that he's going to offer me any clues himself.

I want to talk about his painting. First about color. In the past he had liked the warm toned reds, purples and browns, he was very good at transitional colors, his paintings (in the past) had been mostly interiors, the arrangement of reflected light in a room and the confusing illusions produced by faint candlelight. His copper Tibetan butter tea urns were masterpieces of color. He had liked the use of red by Rembrandt and Caravaggio and other classical masters. But now he had changed, and changed abruptly. Close friends were at a loss over this sudden change. Now, blue was his main tone, there was ultra-marine and turquoise and a grey-blue that resembled the vast skies of Harbin. He had recently acquired a liking for white, silver-white, lead-white and a blueish white but he absolutely would not use that dirty color grey (grey was also a cold tone), he didn't say why. In a word, he had become a painter of pure cold tones. Had his state of mind and perceptions changed?

Next, line. The hitherto gentle, transitional curves at which he had excelled had become perfectly round outlines with little feeling and the paintings often contained irregular, coarse straight lines that did terrifying damage to their visual harmony. His modelling was extremely good and because of his long reverence for the school of realism his change in the use of line gave others greater confidence, the ability to use line to express meaning was no cause for criticism, though at the same time, strictly speaking, it was rather rough.

Next I would like to say something about construction. He did not change the straightforward style of the realists but his construction altered considerably, a somnolent odalisque seemed to become a naked body of pure white, only body hair and the pupil of the eye were black, asleep with the eyes wide open, the skin so realistic that you could touch it; asleep, however, in a transparent rice vinegar bottle. Shanghai Rice Vinegar, with the trademark painted in. Beyond the bottle was a purple *kasaya* tossed casually on the floor with no lama in sight. There was another one, a female nude who seemed to have dropped from heaven, her hair floating elegantly upwards, a dazzling sight, portrayed sitting on a normally painted summit of gold several times larger than her own body. One leg was intentionally bent sideways to conceal her pudenda, and also, so that those parts of her body difficult to manage were covered by its connection with the golden summit. The golden summit seemed bathed in sunlight, the yellow shining white, a large area of blue forming a background that could be imagined as the Lhasa sky.

Fellow artists will say that this is like the Surrealism of Dali, a surface covered by a strange mixture of ultra-realism and abnormality, effulgent but yet ridiculous. I say that it isn't, he is not the same as Dali. He may not be as great as the Spaniard but he is certainly not just duplicating him. I say this not because he is a friend of mine, not at all. If you possessed the curiosity to come to Lhasa and see him you would find out. I'm not making myself clear, after all, I'm a novelist and painting is just a matter of appreciation and of enjoyment.

It looks as if painting took up most of his time. Women could not occupy his creative time. Women were sometimes synonymous with rest. That was a dictum of his. A wonderful story told on a wonderful night.

Was he still dreaming? I don't think it's good.

Only Two People Know

What really intrigued me were the accessories in his studio (workplace) that had no direct connection with his painting but had an extremely close indirect one. A display. To put it another way, the room should have been called a collector's exhibition room (main use) and not a studio (I considered that studio was its secondary function).

To put it in rather more concrete terms, this room was filled with all manner of Tibetan artefacts, works of art and antiques. Leaving aside the money and effort required to amass these objects, the engineering skills required to display them on the walls must have been immense. I had wondered why he had not pushed the easels close against the wall and I had not understood why he had used so much coarse hempen cloth to cover the four walls of the room so tightly, basically I was not curious. The easels, the camp bed and a couple of folding chairs were placed in the center of the room, a very strange way to arrange furniture. Fortunately the room was large and its space allowed him to waste much of the floor area. He only solved this puzzle personally much later, though the intelligent reader will already have realized that the four walls were prolifically hung with his collection.

So it was hung, all of it, on the walls, including a large impressive heavy stone carving. I reckon that the weight of that smiling granite Buddha was not less than that of the man himself. It was all off the ground, suspended, not just in name but in reality, no doubt about it.

The following section is for readers with an interest in the subject, those without an interest in art or archaeology may skip this passage and ignore it. I am going to chart the different categories of his collection, repetitions are not included in the detailed category material.

Stone carvings: Buddhas, human forms, animals (auspicious animals), Buddhas sculpted in relief, ditto animal and human forms, reliefs of inscriptions and incantations from the Tibetan classics, reliefs of various Buddhist designs. Most of the above in color (mineral dyes).

Readymade art statuary: real sheep's head and horns, bharal horns, antelope horns, complete antelope head and horns, tail feathers of a bald eagle, the large branched horns of a red deer, black, white and tea-colored yak's tails.

Handicraft statuary: silver Buddhas, various kinds of bronze Buddhas in different forms, Buddhas made from different colored materials (mud, cloth, silk, rice-straw), card-board Tibetan drama masks, ancient iron helmets, ancient armor, ivory figurines, engraved silver earrings, engraved rings, engraved necklaces and neck ornaments, various kinds of turquoise jewelry, various kinds of red coral jewelry, jade pendants, bronze humans and animals, temple door furniture in iron inlayed with silver, Ming and Qing porcelain and snuff bottles.

Paintings: not many, only two complete and undamaged *thangka* and one damaged. It was a matter of great regret to him that he had no wall paintings.

He said that using modern technology he would certainly find a means of moving some of the Middle Age wall paintings from the ruins of Guge to Lhasa, it was not difficult these days. There was no need for a large quantity, twenty or so square meters would do and with that the room would be complete.

Just now, I deliberately revealed the existence of something amongst the handicraft statuary, a Buddha made of mud. I would like to write about it in a specialist way. This is a sacrificial object commonly seen everywhere in Western Tibet. Along the tops of walls in monasteries and houses, in mountain ravines and on mountain tops and passes where prayer flags are hung. There is basically nothing uncommon about it, his mud Buddha was just a single object amongst an ultimate multiplicity of varieties. There could not have been less than 700 of them, it was the life blood of his travels throughout Tibet. They half-filled the white walls, but it was this single collectors' item alone that dumbfounded and amazed many scholars of Tibet. He had taken a set of color photographs of it, there was only one set of negatives, two sets of reversal film and a number of sets of prints, a set of prints and negatives is said to (I nearly made a slip of the tongue there) be worth tens of thousands of US dollars. It's the only one in the world.

Think of it, when you pulled aside that hemp curtain how ridiculous his oils of bare-bottomed nudes looked amongst the dazzling collection of art on those four wall. He said that the collection in that room encompassed over a thousand years of Tibetan art, he said that although he had not been able to collect the best and the most complete he had already collected the most in number. He also said that in Paris, his collection would be worth at least a billion US dollars! Artists can never forget Paris.

I pride myself that I'm not a bad (rather a good) artist, there's no way that I could fail to be interested in these objects. There was also another reason for my interest (as the sensitive reader will have certainly guessed), so I won't enumerate those base ideas that everybody has, such as envy, jealousy and greed.

I had some anxieties on his account. Every wall has its ears, if the authorities became aware of all this, the consequences would not be difficult to imagine. It was true that he had few friends but he always had women on call, some of whom may have stayed the night, could they not be the cause of a disaster?

He smiled and said: "Women basically don't understand this sort of thing, and I never go after those modern women who like talking about Michelangelo, I like the sort of illiterate women who only understand money and men, I know they're not interested in what's behind the hemp cloth, as far as they're concerned it's just a load of rubbish, besides, I do my utmost to see that they take no interest, so far, not one of them has shown any curiosity about the wall behind the cloth."

"So nobody knows about it?"

"Somebody does, you do."

I felt a sudden cold shiver down my back. I didn't fear him, I was confident that I was more than a match for three like him together, of that I had not the slightest doubt. Then, what was there to be afraid of?

He said: "In fact, many of my acquaintances know that I collect this sort of stuff, but nobody really knows how much I've got and nobody realizes that it's all concentrated here in this room, but you know, do you see?"

I realized at once, I was afraid of knowing a secret that only two people knew, that was it. I suddenly became concerned about the anti-burglar precautions for his studio, but that was superfluous. The large window was fitted with iron bars and it was electrified and he had ordered the three locks on the door from a local locksmith, it was as safe as houses.

The Green Room Western Restaurant

The rumor in Lhasa art circles was that he had sold paintings privately, to a foreigner and at a high price. That I could believe. His paintings could absolutely sell at a high price. High price is an extremely vague concept, how much is high? What are the upper and lower limits? Selling an oil painting for thirty or forty thousand US dollars or in China for three or four thousand yuan is already a high price. The problem is, is the sale legal? There are a whole raft of tax and customs problems. I'd heard that the police were also taking an interest in the matter.

I thought further about that forgotten case and that one-eyed woman. I don't know how I suddenly recalled her and her little courtyard. Then, uninvited, I went to see him, my unexpected visit obviously delighted him. We went to Lhasa's only Green Room Western Restaurant. He said he would be the host.

This restaurant with the rather unpleasant name was doing very good business, perhaps it was its name with its heavy hint of eroticism that brought so many customers intent on fantasy, it was the business knack of the proprietress.

It seemed that this was not the first time that he had been to the Green Room, the proprietress and the staff all knew him well and nodded and greeted him warmly. In truth, none of the three serving staff were young and they were somewhat lacking in appearance and speech. It was difficult to imagine that they ran a restaurant by day and a brothel by night. He tapped casually on the table and the proprietress herself came over, a young woman very capable of inducing fantasies in men. If she received guests herself I guess that the night business would keep up well. With a smile she said that they would bring two portions of French food and he asked for four tins of Qiangli beer. Afterwards he fished out two ten yuan notes and tossed then on the table, I was dumbstruck.

If you go into any restaurant in Lhasa, at the very least it will be 40 or 50 yuan for two, but this was the up-market Green Room! What was 20 yuan good for? However, the proprietress unexpectedly pushed back one of the notes and walked gracefully to the till with the other clasped between her fingertips. I distinctly remember the eroticism of those long rounded fingers, the palms of her hands were small but plump and the fingers slender.

The first course was cream of tomato soup, the table ware was of fine blue patterned china. It was followed by fried chicken. I couldn't manage knife and fork and so used a spoon instead, rather impolitely I finished the tomato soup with a gulp. I wiped my mouth with a napkin and said: "Have you really made a fortune on the side?"

"No way, I painted the sign for this restaurant, and when I come it counts a production cost to them."

"I didn't mean that. Have you really been selling paintings?"

"Rubbish! It's true there was an old American lady who said something about arranging an exhibition for me in America, she said that my paintings would fetch a lot of money. She took some photographs that I had taken of my paintings with her when she left and said she would be in touch. Art circles in Lhasa were in uproar and said that I had sold dozens of paintings. These people have nothing better to do than gossip and make trouble."

"It's said that the police and tax people have been after you?"

"They've seen me. I explained everything to them, they didn't seem too inclined to believe me but they didn't come back. Who knows?"

"No waves without wind, who raised the waves in the first place?"

"Those few comrades of mine, who else? They're envious of me, I paint things they can't, my paintings attract the interest of foreigners, nobody takes any notice of theirs. People! What a business."

"Why no salad?" I asked.

When the proprietress came over again he repeated: "Why no salad? Salami or mixed?" Was this latter addressed to me?

The salad tasted fresh and agreed with me. We then had fried egg and fish steak, pork chops and a beef casserole. Two portions of each. Gradually, we seemed to be unable to keep on eating. When the proprietress came over and asked whether we wanted two portions of dessert I waved my hand indicating that I would do without it. Then, for the first time, the proprietress smiled charmingly at me and said: "This elder brother comes to have a little fun in the evenings, we close at ten."

My confused nod was taken as agreement. When she had gone, I asked him: "Before or after they close?"

He could not hold his drink, his face was red and his tongue rigid as he spoke. "It's up to you, how you under—understand it, great—great author, give vent to your—imagination—nation."

After we left he belched and asked me: "How was it, the food?" And with a hiccup: "All right?"

I pulled him towards the Barkhor. In front of the Jokhang Monastery we turned right, back into the stream of people. It was dusk and the twisting stream of people crowded the Barkhor, we made our way forward in the crowd and were soon squeezed and buffeted by the throng of people. He immediately flared up and started swearing under his breath. I nudged him and said: "This is no place to go looking for trouble." He said: "I wasn't swearing at them, it was at those two ill-begotten bastards." He mumbled the names of his two fellow-students indistinctly.

I dragged him to the fork in the road, the mosque was about two hundred paces ahead, he hadn't realized how close to Wapa Ling he was. He was by no means sober, by contrast I had an idea.

He turned into a public lavatory and I took the opportunity to rush to his house and bang on the door urgently, she came out quickly. Nothing was said and she followed me to the wide alley where he had stopped. We both saw him stagger unsteadily out of the lavatory buttoning up his flies. Her first reaction was to stop, I turned and looked at that single eye, it was filled with tears. I quietly said to her: "Go." And she started walking.

He hadn't seen us, he hadn't seen her.

I called to him and he stopped as well. She stopped for about three seconds and then suddenly dashed forward regardless and seized his arm. I saw the look of surrender on his face and at once turned tactfully homeward.

I did not see him for a while and thought that he had of course gone home to be a dutiful husband. But I think that I must have been to see him once during this time. As I recollect, the two *thangka* in his workplace studio were not the two that the old man had been working on before he had laid down his brush for ever. I could not be certain whether or not they were also by the hand of that old master. There had been too many Tibetan objects dazzling my eyes that night and I hadn't had the time to examine the *thangka* closely, in retrospect I had been utterly stupid. I remembered that he had told me that the old man still retained eleven of his own paintings. Perhaps there were only nine still left at her house? I really am a detective story writer.

He appeared again without waiting for me to go and see him. He was in a good mood and was fatter and paler. As if he knew what I was thinking, he at once pulled a small photo album from his pocket, they were standard colored prints, all of *thangka*. "Twelve paintings altogether. Look, this is the unfinished one that you saw, it looks complete. The composition is all there, it's only the fine detail of portrayal that is lacking. Haven't you heard that Leonardo Da Vinci took over four years to paint the Mona Lisa? He painted and repainted a single fingernail thirty times. The old man's technique was perfect, Leonardo couldn't equal him. In the realms of the sublime, magic in every brushstroke. The pity is that he believed in Buddha, if he had believed in Jehovah it would have been different."

I said: "Not necessarily." He twisted my meaning. "You mean he's not as good as Leonardo? Don't you understand? Look at this brushwork, look at this and this, take a look, take a good look ..."

I said: "I said that believing in Jehovah was not necessarily better than believing in Sakyamuni. Buddhism and Protestantism and Roman Catholicism …"

"All right, all right, that's getting away from the subject. All these paintings are late works of his and worth more than his early work."

"What really was it about his death?" I had finally found an opportunity, and decided to go for the jugular. What I said demolished his good humor, it was the only way to get results.

He remained tight-lipped for a long time, I thought I would have to break the deadlock.

"His death was a great pity, even if he had already finished that great painting …" I looked carefully at the expression on his face.

He still didn't respond. I could only withdraw. "I still think that the two paintings in your studio are the master's."

This time he emerged from the labyrinth. "No, I got them myself, two hundred years old, the tattered one is even older, I hear it's Ming dynasty."

"Do you live at work or at home?"

"Both. Two days at home and a day at work, if I don't go home she comes looking for me the next morning."

I still didn't understand. "Then why do you have stay over at work? Aren't you and your wife now on good terms?"

He said: "How little you know, you needn't think just because you are married … Han women and Tibetans are not the same."

"I hear they're very passionate."

"Those who eat meat are not the same as those who eat grass."

"Was this the reason you and your wife lived apart a while ago?"

My attempts to seek an opening had all failed and the conversation had been brought to a halt by his sudden silence. As he was about to leave he suddenly spoke up and caught me unawares with a single question.

"Have you been to the Green Room again?"

He clearly noticed my agitation and then smiled happily. As he went out of the door he winked towards the inner room, I maintained an expression of "what else can I do?" At that moment my wife called from the inner room: "Has he gone?"

The White Witch

Events developed rapidly.

It was my wife who heard first. She heard her colleagues at the newspaper office discussing the arrest of a foreign woman by the police, they'd heard that the woman had kicked up a terrible fuss, they didn't know whether or not she had been released in the end.

"Released? No way! If they release her, it'll strengthen her case, why not take it to Beijing?"

"Hard to say, if she's not released what then? There's nothing illegal, I wonder at the lack of care of the police in making the arrest."

"Nothing illegal? Adultery with a married man?"

"What adultery? He wasn't arrested, it was the model."

"Models are naked then?"

"You've obviously never been in an art college studio, so many people clustered round a naked model painting, when did a model ever wear clothes?"

"Whatever you say, she was there overnight."

"Painting overnight. Why didn't you say so?"

"A lot of nights?"

"If there was a lot of overnight painting that means there must be paintings, completed oil paintings would be evidence."

"When the police knocked on the door and announced themselves he didn't dare delay and opened it at once, he was clothed and the woman was wrapped in a blanket with nothing on underneath. It was five o'clock in the morning and still dark, they say the foreigner had been mixed in there with the artist for several days and nights, his unit really couldn't face it any more and reported it. Serve him right. Bad luck on the artist."

"Didn't they say he'd been released the same day?"

"He was. I heard the foreign woman hasn't left and is demanding an explanation from the police and that they must compensate her. They say that abroad, infringement of human rights is compensated with a lot of money."

"A great deal. But you have to take it to court and win."

"It's called winning a case."

"They say the artist's wife is one-eyed, lives in a turning off Wapa Ling."

"I've seen her, a one-eyed woman who often does her vegetable shopping at Tromsikhang market. About thirty, medium height."

"The artist is much younger than she is, rather good looking."

"Is he Han?"

"Yes, there's not much inter-marriage between Tibetans and Han these days."

"There was a lot in the past."

"She went there to plead with the artist too, it seems relations between the two are not bad at all."

My wife came home and expounded the comments of her colleagues to me, it was quite clear that he had got himself into trouble.

"He's finished! Getting mixed up with a foreigner for what? Isn't he afraid of catching Aids? Each and every foreigner smells, it makes you sick." So my wife concluded.

I thought that perhaps there were other reasons. "Might he not have been thinking of selling a few pictures through her? Or selling some of his Tibetan collection?"

"He's asking for trouble, it's the death penalty for selling cultural objects, you'll have to talk to him, he'll still listen to you. He's not a bad man in himself, he's just too greedy and conscious of money."

I knew that it was crisis time for him, going to see him

might arouse the attention of the police but he very much needed a good friend to talk things over with. I decided to visit his house.

I said previously that I had never had another opportunity to visit the little courtyard, it was because I took the old route through the Barkhor and without much difficulty came across him out sketching. Sketching in oil. I couldn't conceive that he could be out sketching with his portfolio on his back in the most crowded part of Lhasa after such a serious event. He must be as cool as a cucumber and capable of coping with anything.

I hesitated at first, perhaps there were plain-clothes police on patrol nearby. I walked over and greeted him. He turned to look at me and said, very normally, "You've come," and then resumed his concentration on his painting.

I didn't know what to say and so just stood there behind him, watching his brush going back and forth across the oil painting. He didn't turn round and just occasionally said something to indicate that he was not cold shouldering me, I saw no point in standing there and said: "I'm going."

He grunted "Ah" and went on to say: "At this time of day, the setting sun turns everything yellow, such a beautiful golden yellow!" He was painting the golden eaves of the Jokhang Monastery, they were a pale golden white, but now the whole of Lhasa was a sheet of warm gold, a subjective color, too subjective.

As I left I tossed out the phrase: "When you've finished painting come and have supper at home, it's fried noodles." Again, he grunted "Ah."

After she was released, the foreign woman became even more abandoned. It was the time of the Tibetan Bathing Festival and to the astonishment of all Lhasa she went to Sunshine Island in the Lhasa River every evening after supper to bathe naked. One evening after supper I told my wife that we should go and have a look. She said that she was just thinking of going to see some fun and as we left the sun hadn't yet touched the tips of the western hills.

Sunshine Island was also called Robber's Wood and is separated from the shore by a narrow current of water, a steel wire suspension bridge connects the island to Lhasa city on the north bank. Normally it was deserted but now it was the scene of unprecedented excitement. We could see from a distance that the bank was crowded and that many of them had made their way onto the bridge which was seething with people.

Across from the bank, on the island, was a smooth, bright, sandy beach, almost like an open air theater with the audience applauding from the river bank. She really was standing there on the sand without a stitch on, blowing three rounds of kisses to the surrounding onlookers, she was young, her voluptuous body a dazzling white. Like a dancer she kicked her legs left and right as if deliberately exposing her pudenda, fortunately at this point the setting sun slipped perfectly behind the hills. Then like an athlete warming up she exercised her waist and legs and gingerly entered the foaming water with slow steps until she was waist deep. On the surface of the water her breasts looked as if sculpted from fine white porcelain. No flash photography missed the opportunity and many young people applauded the sight.

To avoid the suspicion of naturalism I cannot write in more detail. Even my wife said in a low voice: "She's got something." There was nothing else I could say and I just said: "She's got a good figure."

She amused herself in the water for a long time until the darkness enveloped her, we didn't wait for her to emerge and get dressed, and walked back home.

I got out the yellow notebook again tonight and sat in the lamplight for a long time. I hesitated long before including the white witch.

Everyday Scare Tactics

This time, it was no longer rumor. First discovered by the customs, then reported to the police and immediately taken into custody. It was she who came and told me and said that before it was dark she heard police cars arriving, the sound of the sirens was terrifying. There were five policemen armed with electric batons and she also saw one who seemed to be in command whose hand rested on his pistol holster. She was scared stiff, a Tibetan policeman told her in Tibetan: "It's none of your business."

I asked: "Did they say why he was being taken away?"

"Yes, they said he had been selling national treasures—what's a national treasure?"

Hell! He really had committed a crime. He must have sold some cultural relics and been caught. I knew that this time it was no small matter and I regretted not having listened to my wife and not having been to see him and warn him in time.

Her single eye was filled with distress and my mind was uneasy. I made her go home and said that I would think what to do and make enquiries, if there was any news I would come and tell her.

There was still no opportunity to re-visit that courtyard, she came seeking news every evening at supper time. By the third day without news she was really beginning to annoy me. She didn't come at the same time on the fourth day and I had had no news at all. My wife said: "They've held the news of this arrest very tight, there's nothing at all going the rounds and it's been some days now, not a shred of news." We thought that we would eat supper in peace. The electricity went off as usual at night and probably wouldn't resume until some time after midnight. I had just lit a candle when he and his one-eyed wife walked into our little courtyard together. He was back.

He seemed paler but in good spirits. He knew that we would have been anxious about him and so had come to set our minds at rest straight away. Without waiting for me to ask, he described the affair from start to finish.

Two years earlier he had visited a ruined temple in the southern hills to do some sketching. It was a very small temple, most of its structure had collapsed and only some ruined walls were left standing at the top of a small hill. Communications were poor in the extreme and there was no large inhabited area nearby. He heard of it by word of mouth and found his way there by asking. He took some dried food with him, he was accustomed to hardship.

Needless to say, he was delighted when he saw the ruins on the distant hilltop. He had a sleeping bag and two Tibetan swords, one long one short. He decided to camp in the ruins.

Contrary to his expectations the temple was not a complete ruin, two unoccupied buildings remained, probably used by herdsmen as resting places. There was cow dung and wood ash, it looked like a fire, either for keeping warm or for cooking. There were neither doors nor windows but the door and window frames were still relatively complete.

He camped in one of the buildings for about a fortnight. Each day, he exchanged daily necessities with local herdsmen for objects that came from the temple, small bronze Buddhas, vases and jars, bronze incense burners and so on. He said that he did not get much this way. He remembered that on the way back he carried a can of fresh water on his back to moisten the dried compressed biscuit to make it edible.

During the day, bald eagles used the hill as a place to sun-bathe and the stone walls were covered with white eagle droppings. After he arrived the eagles ceased to land on the hill but circled low and menacingly, their dark shadows passing over the sunlit ruins again and again. It was only the eagles that kept him company during those days.

His real find was in the two buildings. He found no temple treasure or sacrificial objects. It was only when he rubbed away the thick smoke deposit on the walls that he realized his discovery—wall paintings!

Inch by inch he photographed the surface of the paintings in close-up. Then he sat and copied the originals of the paintings that he particularly liked. His basic technique was sound and his copies could almost be taken for the originals—he used poster color as a medium and the color was objective, he was certain that this was a pre-Ming wall painting, perhaps Song, he was, of course, very familiar with the various styles of ancient painting. So, bit by bit, he tore up his shirt and rubbed the wall clean and photographed and copied the painting. The days passed quickly, he was in a desperate situation, at the point where he had not a copper on him, when there was not a crumb of biscuit left in his pack and when he had run out of camera film he was obliged to give up and leave.

This was a truly significant home-coming loaded with the spoils of victory.

"The photographs weren't a problem. It was the paintings that I had copied. After that old American lady I told you about went home, another pair of Americans arrived, both China experts and introduced by the old lady. They came to find me and look at paintings. I discovered that they weren't interested in my paintings, that was disappointing. They were only interested in the copies that I had made of the wall paintings. They asked me whether I would sell."

I saw that it was going to be a long story and my wife made coffee for everybody. Shanghai coffee, to which ladies add a sugar-cube.

"I said at the time that I wouldn't sell and then regretted it. I could always make another copy but I didn't say anything. They came again after a few days and I didn't say anymore. They offered a high price. I said I wasn't selling, they said they didn't understand and I said that I needed a decent camera for painting and they immediately said no problem."

They wanted to see the paintings at once, he said not. They probably thought that he would change his mind. They said they thought it best if they took the paintings with them this time and that when they got back they would immediately invite him to America and they would meet the expenses.

He cared most for what he had already gained and for the photographic equipment.

It was a Canon-E, a world class brand, a three-year-old model with a standard 1.4 lens, a 16–80 mm medium to wide angle lens and a 70–200 mm telephoto lens as well as two extender lenses.

He was an expert photographer and knew that the standard price of this set of photographic equipment in a state-run store would be not less than 7,000 yuan. It was difficult to estimate the value of his copies of the wall paintings but he felt that he could make something of the situation.

He then let them look at the wall paintings that he had originally not intended them to see again. He took especial notice of the ones in which they showed particular interest. There were seven copies in all of the wall paintings, each about 70 cm square. He then took back the paintings and said what he thought.

"I said, that if they left me the camera they could take three, I said I was not open to discussion, they whispered amongst themselves and said that they had some US dollars with them and they would like to take five paintings, leaving me all the photographic equipment and 700 US dollars. At once I said four paintings. I gave them no room for maneuver and they just had to accept. They wanted to choose but I didn't let them, I chose three to keep and let them take the rest."

Three days later the customs and police came for him and took him to an isolation cell in the customs building. He was not excessively ill-treated, they just asked him to give a truthful account of events. They wanted a written account. To start with, he thought about whether or not he should conceal the fact that he had received the camera and foreign currency but then he thought that the Americans may have already mentioned it and decided to conceal nothing and wrote an account many pages long. He stayed there several days and was fed for free.

I asked: "Why did they take you to the customs?"

He said: "Probably because there were no legal contradictions. If they had arrested me and handed me to the judicial authorities before they had clarified the situation it would have been difficult to handle later. In this case, they could say that I had been taken to the customs in order to clarify the situation."

"It's not the same. They didn't let you go home and there were police there exerting pressure."

"I didn't say that they wouldn't let me go home. I didn't think of asking to be allowed home. It involved foreigners and who is to say that the police should not assist the customs in understanding the situation? It's difficult to be clear about whether or not the police exerted pressure, they didn't hit anybody or swear at them."

"It was clearly mental pressure."

"You could say that it was also a case of guilty conscience. If you haven't done anything to be ashamed of you shouldn't be alarmed at a knock on the door in the middle of the night. Why should there be any mental pressure?"

I knew that there was something in what he said. The sense of something could only be sensed, it was impossible to spell it out. Impossible to describe in words. The Chinese approach to psychology.

I asked: "What was the conclusion?"

"They said it was not permitted to trade privately with foreigners, especially in the export of prohibited items, reproductions included. There are no detailed national regulations in this area."

"Couldn't you have said that reproductions of the *Mona Lisa* are popular throughout the world? That museums abroad allow everybody to copy and photograph their most famous paintings?"

"Haven't I had enough? Aren't I in enough trouble? I've broken the national foreign currency administration rules and so forth, neither the tax authorities nor the customs permit this sort of trade. The four remaining paintings are with the customs awaiting processing. I've also had to give back the photographic equipment and the US currency, they will hand it over to the foreigners. They said I should study the law carefully, so that I had a mental concept of the law, that although I was a graduate I was legally blind. I agreed enthusiastically, yes, yes, yes ..."

I said: "I once went through a red traffic light at an

NO SAIL ON THE WESTERN SEA

intersection. The traffic policeman confiscated my bicycle and made me pay 50 cents for a stenciled traffic regulations leaflet to study. Did they sell you a copy of *Legal General Knowledge* or anything?"

"No. They said that if artists wished to sell their pictures they should do so through the relevant state organization, in a proper process where tax is paid when necessary and applications made to customs when required."

"Unfortunately you don't quite have the qualifications. If it were the paintings of Qi Baishi or Pan Tianshou[1] it would be a different matter. Drink your coffee."

Object before Verb

We've arrived at the final moments of the hero of this story. The so-called end. The so called object. In the subject-verb-object pattern I have decided to put the object first and to reveal the ending to the reader in this chapter. That is to say, this chapter should originally have been the last.

To clarify a little, this is not the last chapter, it's the end; the final chapter is not the end. I am being repetitious.

After they left I carried on drinking coffee with my wife and we continued to talk about it all.

My wife thought that he had messed it up by accepting the American dollars, it would have been much simpler if it had merely been an exchange of items and he had not accepted the money. Her theory was that like this, there was no buying or selling, it was a mutual exchange of gifts, the making of gifts was not illegal. The most that could be said was that certain things were not suitable as gifts for foreigners, the tone of this conclusion was a great deal more tactful.

---

1   Qi Baishi (1864–1957) and Pan Tianshou (1897–1971) were well known 20th century Chinese artists.—Trans.

I believed that it was not quite so simple. The problem was that it had got into the hands of the customs who had then handed it to the police, so that whether or not there was an offence it was still rather troublesome. It was now certain that they were copies, that conclusion was the best so far. I even considered that there was no need to ask for the four pictures back, if they were returned it meant that they had been taken for nothing, if they were not then it had been a waste of time. She strongly believed that this was not so.

"On what grounds do they not give them back? When artists in the interior copy wall paintings from ruined buildings they are rescuing national historical relics, on what grounds can the state confiscate them? If they go on like this nobody will look after this sort of thing, wouldn't that be a complete waste?"

"So they could give it away to foreigners?"

"It comes to the same thing, foreigners are not going to take it and destroy it, and in the end this bit of humanity's cultural heritage will be preserved."

"But the state loses its right to protect it."

"As he said, he can make another copy."

It was all mere talk, whether it was him or my wife.

It seemed that the white witch who had bathed naked had a real interest in him. When she got back to Australia (she was an Australian of Scottish descent) she had immediately arranged lectures, exhibitions and tours for him. The Australian Department of Culture had written formally to the Chinese Ministry of Culture inviting the famous young Chinese artist in Lhasa (no name mentioned) on a year-long lecture tour of three Australian art institutes together with a one man exhibition at the gallery of the Sydney College of the Arts and other visits to fourteen major Australian cities, etc., etc.

I don't know why it is that all the little men of Lhasa that I write about want to emigrate? According to what they say themselves, they are determined not to accept transfers to Beijing, Shanghai, Guangzhou or Chengdu, I won't go into the reasons here. I don't agree with the view that my generation of intellectuals is in love with the West, at the very least I'm not, I'm certainly not prepared to bow before any living foreign author.

It seemed that he had to make a special visit to Beijing to undertake formalities and to go to the Australian embassy, in Lhasa he also had to go through additional procedures at a number of departments. In his own words, his legs were worn thin with dashing about. He had originally thought that it would not be easy to get away but in the end nobody stood in his way. He said it was because of the attractions that lay outside. Perhaps the scent of flowers beyond the wall can be smelled inside.

The Tibetan news organizations ceaselessly publicized him. He became an ideal figure seeking glory for the nation. He was on television, I heard that he came over well, at ease and fluent in his answers, quite the great man, the poised master. Unfortunately I don't have a television.

He was busy all the time and never showed his face, when he did come, it was the evening of the day before his plane took off. He was smartly dressed in a western suit and even his wife was wearing a colorful new Tibetan costume. An important personage who, naturally, could not be too casual in his attire.

"They're sending a car for me at the crack of dawn tomorrow to take me to the airport." When he said "they," his tone was one of obvious contempt.

"What about the paintings?"

"It's all done. They've been crated and will be delivered to the airport in the morning to follow on."

"Then," I hesitated a moment, "then the things at your workplace, what are you doing about them?"

"I've spent the last few days dealing with them, they've all been moved to the house, there was enough to move, I spent a lot of money."

"Why didn't you give me a call?" Ingratiating myself after the event.

"The busy great author. I thought I would spend some

money on hiring people and a vehicle to do the moving. I didn't dare trouble you."

"Bloody fool."

I saw that my wife and his were talking in an undertone and lowered my voice too. "Did she, arrange it for you? I hear her father's the Australian deputy foreign minister, is that right?"

Equally in an undertone: "That's right, when she left she said she wanted to get me to Australia, I didn't think it would be so quick."

"Then you won't go to America?"

"Not the slightest sign of anything there. In any case it's much easier to get to America from Australia."

"Will she make you come back?"

"Who knows. If I don't want to come back, then I'll take permanent residence."

"Then how will your wife manage? She looks out of sorts."

"She hasn't said a thing these last few days, she hasn't said a word at home, I'm on the point of exploding. Yes, she made me move the things from my workspace back to the house, she said that she knew that there was a lot of valuable stuff there, I asked her how she knew, she said better to move it back, it would be safer. She also said that she knew that those things were my life. She's never been to my workspace. It's bloody strange."

"Will you move back? I think she's afraid that you won't come back and will use those things to haul you back, you're in a trap."

"That's up to her, for my part, I've no mind to divorce, without a divorce that stuff is still mine. Her mind's set on staying with me, she's devoted, of that I'm absolutely certain."

"What happens if you get there and that one wants to marry you?"

"'If the boat reaches the pier the way is straight.' If there's no bigamy agreement between the two countries we'll marry, if there is and I have to divorce here before marrying there, we'll see when the time comes. Who can say what may happen in the future. Perhaps I may want to marry the one there and she won't.

I say, say whatever whenever, what do you think?"

It looked as if he had thought it through and rather more thoroughly than I had.

I had been anxious to no purpose.

My wife and I saw them to the gate of the Jokhang Monastery, I wished him a safe journey and said that if there were any difficulties he could always call on me. When he had gone some distance he turned and waved.

His plane took off at eleven o'clock the following morning, stopped at Chengdu for an hour and a half and carried on to Beijing. He stayed at the Mongolia Hotel on one of Beijing's broad streets that night and on the morning of the fourth day China Airlines international 747 flight to Sydney took off. On the night of that day, a house in Lhasa's old city caught fire. Because it was discovered late and also because the narrow alleys surrounding the house prevented the fire engines getting to it, by the time the fire was out at first light, the house had been completely burnt down. The firemen were only able to recover a few sculpted stone Buddhas from the ashes and on that basis concluded that the occupants of the house had been Buddhists. The neighbors did not know much about this single-gated courtyard but did know that a one-eyed woman frequently went in and out, she was about thirty and of medium build. The imposing willow tree in the courtyard had been burnt bare of its leaves.

To my mind, there is something not quite right about the end of this story. I originally tried to alter the ending, I had always prided myself on my ability to handle several different possibilities but in the end I suddenly changed my mind, the reasons were complicated and impossible to explain in just a word or two.

I then began to build the principal idea of the novel into its construction. I deliberately put the story of the murder of the old master artist, which the reader (a lot of readers) wanted very much to see solved, at the end. I have no place in this story. I also think I should say that it's a terrifying story of love.

I remember the yellow notebook and the attempt by the

nonsensical author who believed himself infallible to lead the reader to a fork in the road. Think for a moment, what madman would haul back the sun from the west and push it back into the sea of Japan in the east? Facts are more factual than any fantasy.

I don't know how I should revisit the murder of the old master of painting in the middle section of this novel. I think I will use the simplest and most straightforward method. Turn back, turn back to the part where the old master first appeared.

Retelling the Tale of the Virtuous Woman

I

When the police car arrived at the scene, hardly anybody noticed the woman walking slowly along the road that bordered the river beach. The lower half of her face was tightly swathed in a green headscarf and her head was lowered. There was a chill to the early spring wind and it was all accompanied by the shrill sound of police sirens.

In this sequence of events she reached the scene a step ahead of the police car. It was the police siren and the severe looking police uniforms that had caused her to stop. Then the police car had arrived, juddering to a halt as two formidable looking policemen threw open its doors as soon as its wheels stopped turning, their high leather boots crunching across the shingle. At this point she was standing in the middle of a thicket of willows some 60 paces away.

Including the driver, five policemen in peaked caps stood over that unrecognizable corpse. One had a camera and another in white gloves was a forensic investigator. Three black crows flew low overhead calling as they went. The forensic investigator said lugubriously: "Those crows scooped out the stomach."

It was then that she came over. Only a Tibetan policeman heard what she said but he was hesitantly uncertain.

"She spoke Tibetan, she seemed to say—*Ba* (dad)—or —*Po*

(a term of address for an old man), the wind was blowing through the willows, I can't say for certain that that was what she said. Perhaps it was the noise of the wind."

"I'm certain that I saw that she had only one eye, although her face was wrapped in a scarf, I'm sure I couldn't be mistaken. She closed her eye for quite a while, for about two or three seconds?"

At the time, the police did not think to ask her: "Do you know the deceased?" or "Who are you? Where do you live?" and just let her go.

The nearest milestone had the figure 23 on it, it was 23 km from Lhasa city. The flesh had separated from the bones of the corpse just leaving a very few strips of flesh hanging there, as if vultures and crows had already pecked and fed from it, a sight too horrible to contemplate. When the left arm, pressed down under one side of the body was turned over, a spiral gold ring of four loops could be seen on the bottom joint of the middle finger of the hand. The thickness of the middle finger joint prevented the ring being removed easily, the joint had to be snapped in two. When removed the ring became a strip of yellow gold several centimeters long. It provided no clue. There were at least 8,000 rings of this sort in Lhasa.

II

He was able to enjoy the love of his wife. She labored all day from morn till night without a moment's rest. Shopping and cooking but mainly waiting on that grotesque old man. She was an only daughter, the father was semi-paralyzed and waiting on him was an inescapable duty.

The old man was upstairs, his daily routine of eating and drinking, urinating and defecating was conducted upstairs and arranged and cleared up by her, he never came down. She spent six or seven hours each day at his side. His temperament was perverse, he never spoke to his son-in-law and normally did not allow him upstairs, if he wished to come upstairs he had to obtain his father-in-law's agreement through his wife. The son-in-law had thought that this was a matter of racial differences. The son-in-law was Han and like his father-in-law, an artist. The father-in-law, a master of *thangka* painting. The son-in-law had studied oil painting at art school and had become an art editor after arriving in Tibet, he also painted watercolors.

The old man always went to bed late and his daughter had to see him off to sleep before she came downstairs, by which time her husband was usually asleep. The old man did not sleep much and woke early, his daughter had to rise early to attend to him and, as a result, neglected her vigorous young husband. A thirty-year-old male who everyday went to bed and slept in dreamland without the company of his wife and whose wife had already left by the time he emerged from his dreams, how long could this be endured?

His moments of intimacy with his wife occurred when he burned with desire and so could not sleep. Normally, he got through a lot of work in a day and was tired, it was not often that he could not get to sleep. There was another detail that he had noticed, his wife had never kissed him and had never let him kiss her. He had thought that Tibetans did not like this intangible sexual activity and had thought no more of it. Lengthy sexual starvation reminded him of the scented wild flowers of his bachelor days.

III

He was beginning to be at his wit's end over his wife's sudden bouts of weeping. In normal circumstances, they had very little interaction on a spiritual plane and he had no conception of what she thought, though he sensed that she loved him deeply. When he was painting she could watch him fixedly for hours on end, not what he was painting but he himself. This wordless depth of feeling needed no commentary, a look was enough. Moreover, he was her husband and after a while he became accustomed to these sudden tears and accepted them as in no way out of the ordinary.

When he painted her his concentration was intense but there were always rests and she liked his excitement then, the true strength of attraction in women lies in their constant ability to stimulate desire in their husbands. In turn, she immersed herself passionately in the rainstorm of his love. Thereafter the creation of the artistic masterpiece continued.

He realized that her bouts of crying were becoming more frequent.

That night he was fast asleep but was wakened by the sound of her crying. She didn't sleep but sat at his side caressing him as she sobbed gently. He woke but didn't open his eyes and lay there with his eyes closed until he fell asleep again.

IV

"I know you have women at your workplace as well."

"They're models. How do you know anyhow?"

"Do you rest when you paint them too?"

"Well, no, sometimes, it's not all resting."

"I don't blame you. I blame myself, it's all my fault."

"What's your fault? Artists can't always paint the same person, the feeling would be lifeless. Do you understand 'lifeless'?"

"It's my fault. I don't blame you."

"I've never blamed you."

"I blame myself, not you."

"You've been crying a lot recently."

"I blame myself, I'm not good. I don't want to cry. I know you don't like me crying. I can't bear it, then I cry."

"It doesn't matter, cry if you want to, it eases the mind, if you don't cry when you're upset, it can make you ill."

"I won't always cry, I won't always be bad."

"What are you talking about?"

"Truly, I won't always be like this. And I know why you married me."

"Don't be idiotic."

"I know you like those *thangka* of his."

"Of course I do. He's a great artist and I hope to learn something about painting from him."

"I know it's not that, you married me for the paintings. I'm happy I can give them to you."

"I don't know what nonsense you're talking?"

"I know that you don't want me to know all this. I know you are thinking of something. You're thinking that he should die a little before his time."

"Heavens, what are you thinking of, are you feverish?"

V

He sensed that there was something wrong.

That evening, he said that he was feeling out of sorts, his head ached and he went to bed first. After he was asleep she went upstairs a little later than normal. He then got up and crept up the staircase, the door of the old man's room was still open, she came out with the chamber pot and he quickly hid behind a pillar. It was dark and she didn't discover him, she emptied the chamber pot next to the lavatory downstairs and returned to the room closing the door. Time passed and when he was certain that she would not come out again he tip-toed forward.

The door fitted tightly and there was no keyhole or other cracks through which he could spy, it was tightly closed. He noticed a shaft of candlelight under the door. He decided to lie prone on the floor, he intended to find out why she had said what she had and why she was always crying.

For over an hour he lay at the foot of that rough wooden door and came to understand a tragedy of utter inhumanity.

She first lowered the back of his chair to form a bed where he reclined in comfort. She thereupon, naked from the waist down, straddled his face letting him perform an obscenity. He could not see the expression on the old man's face and felt only a stomach churning wish to vomit. He saw that her eyes were closed in an appearance of apathetic indifference. After a long time the old man appeared satisfied and she dismounted and put on her trousers. She then took off the old man's trousers, covered him in a blanket and finally knelt and used her mouth.

He realized why she would not let him kiss her and never kissed him. In the circumstances, he also realized why she made sure the old man was asleep before she could come down stairs again. He did not wish her to realize that he now knew all of this and so went downstairs first. He did not sleep all that night but lay motionless with his eyes closed. She sat and caressed him and wept and finally went to sleep.

VI

He said nothing and moved to his workplace studio. He had a studio at his unit and put up a camp bed which he covered with the bedding that he had used as a bachelor. He was deeply depressed and wanted to talk to somebody. He found the author Big Ma, unfortunately a friend of his had just died and the death of this friend, crushed to death as he was, had seemed to disturb Big Ma mentally. Whatever he said Big Ma had taken as referring to Thondup (the friend in question). There was nothing he could do. As a result he came and went in a cloud of depression, returning to the studio to a confused sleep.

Later he learned that his father-in-law was missing and later still heard from her that her father was dead, he had met her in the Barkhor. She had said nothing more after she told him and had not even asked him to come home.

He also heard that in late spring and early summer, Big Ma had travelled widely, he heard that he had displayed a deep interest in places that he himself had visited and had made a special record of things that he had done. Big Ma had never asked him anything, had he done so, he would have told him everything. Big Ma was, it could be said, his only intimate friend.

He also thought that Big Ma may have thought that he had killed somebody, but there had been no opportunity to explain. There was no silver hidden here1, no lessons to be learned from the past.

Eventually, he invited Big Ma to his studio. Big Ma had only appeared interested in his collection and his latest works, Big Ma, it seemed, was no great dreamer and was not much given to fantasy. He and Big Ma had had a western meal together, he had drunk too much and Big Ma had taken him home to Wapa Ling. He didn't know when Big Ma had left, he believed that Big Ma and his one-eyed baby wife had conspired together and got him home by deceit.

VII

That evening was the first time that he and his wife had been alone together in the house and it made them rather uncomfortable. Mainly because they were not used to it. In a break with habit she served beer.

This was his second lot of beer in a day. Normally he never drank alcohol more than three times a year, limited to beer of course.

Half drunk, he said to her: "Big Ma definitely believes that I killed the old man."

She said: "I can explain to him."

"What's the point of explaining? The more you explain the worse it gets and the false becomes true. Do you know why they say 'There's no three hundred ounces of silver here[1]'?"

How could she know? "No, I don't."

Having drunk the last of the beer he slumped down. He had drunk too much.

She arranged the bed, undressed him, covered him with a quilt and sat beside the bed in a daze for a long time. He woke up and saw her sitting there staring into the distance, at once he was sober and alert.

She said: "Don't get cold, lie down, lie down."

He had to lie down again.

"Lie down and listen to me."

He said: "You don't have to tell me."

She said: "I must. Then you will understand."

---

1   An allusion to the story of the peasant who buried 300 ounces of silver and in order to prevent it being stolen posted a notice saying "There's no 300 ounces of silver here." His neighbor promptly stole it and left a note denying that he had done so. Used to indicate a very poor lie that reveals the truth.—Trans.

He said: "I think I understand already."

She said: "It's definitely not what you think it is."

He said: "The Han call it incest."

She said: "I know you got it wrong."

He said: "I saw it all. Really disgusting."

She said: "I know. You were bound to find out sooner or later, there was nothing wrong in you seeing."

He said: "I don't know. Perhaps you think there's nothing wrong in this. I'm Han, I don't know."

She said: "He was Han as well. He was in Lhasa from a child, in the Potala. He hated the Han, I don't understand. He wasn't my father."

He said: "What do you mean, not your father?"

She said: "I was his woman, I was his woman from the time I was small. I know he was Han, he hated the Han."

Heavens, oh heavens, oh—

VIII

The next evening they changed the subject.

She said: "Let's start again."

He said: "Then let's start again."

IX

Of course, she was making up for it but he couldn't stomach it.

Sometimes he hid in the studio, she was certain to come and take him home the next day. He was as obedient as a lamb, obedient to her orders.

X

She heard the news of his invitation to Australia and ate nothing for a day. She told him that she knew that it was that white woman who wanted him to go. She didn't say "You mustn't go."

He though that she was just a little jealous and thought no more of it.

Later she urged him to move everything in the studio back

home and the workplace and the studio at home were combined into one.

The night before he left, he and his wife visited the home of Big Ma the author together and stayed until late. She paid attention to everything in his low-voiced conversation with Big Ma.

XI

"I want to tell you something, I killed the old man."

"I guessed as much long ago. The old man couldn't move, was it you that carried him to the Lhasa River?"

"I was exhausted. I was really tired then."

"It was enough for you to carry, he was so tall and so fat."

"You don't want to know why I killed him?"

"Why?"

"Never mind, there's no why."

"I think I know why. It was for me, wasn't it?"

"I ... love you too."

"I would do anything for you."

"Ha ..."

He yawned, he was sleepy.

He said: "Time for bed, I have to get up early tomorrow."

XII

In the morning he ate the egg that she had cooked and then the car arrived.

XIII

There is no thirteen.

Stories by Contemporary Writers from Shanghai

The Little Restaurant
Wang Anyi

A Pair of Jade Frogs
Ye Xin

Forty Roses
Sun Yong

Goodby, Xu Hu!
Zhao Changtian

Vicissitudes of Life
Wang Xiaoying

The Elephant
Chen Cun

Folk Song
Li Xiao

The Messenger's Letter
Sun Ganlu

Ah, Blue Bird
Lu Xing'er

His One and Only
Wang Xiaoyu

When a Baby Is Born
Cheng Naishan

Dissipation
Tang Ying

Paradise on Earth
Zhu Lin

Beautiful Days
Teng Xiaolan

The Most Beautiful Face in the World
Xue Shu

Between Confidantes
Chen Danyan

She She
Zou Zou

There Is No If
Su De

Calling Back the Spirit of the Dead
Peng Ruigao

White Michelia
Pan Xiangli

Platinum Passport
Zhu Xiaolin

Game Point
Xiao Bai

Memory and Oblivion
Wang Zhousheng

Labyrinth of the Past
Zhang Yiwei

No Sail on the Western Sea
Ma Yuan

Gone with the River Mist
Yao Emei

The Confession of a Bear
Sun Wei